VICIOUS CIRCLE

VICIOUS CIRCLE

Hope For A Brighter Future

MARGIE GARRETT

authorHOUSE®

AuthorHouse™
1663 Liberty Drive
Bloomington, IN 47403
www.authorhouse.com
Phone: 1-800-839-8640

First published by AuthorHouse   06/06/2011

ISBN: 978-1-4634-1155-8 (sc)
ISBN: 978-1-4634-1154-1 (dj)
ISBN: 978-1-4634-1153-4 (ebk)

Library of Congress Control Number: 2011908631

Printed in the United States of America

CONTENTS

REVIEWS

"The author captures what I have perceived to be "right on" regarding the trials and tribulations of the dating world. It is so difficult to trust once you have been hurt. I felt the pain she has endured by the way she conveyed her story, and could relate too many of the dating situations. I also learned from this book, things not to do. I highly recommend this book for anyone who has suffered a loss in love and attempts to regain their own identity as they set out in the world of relationships again. Though I haven't experienced the illness or depression to the degree of the author, I felt the daily struggles and setbacks she had, as she dealt with her adversities."

Rosemarie Menosky

INTRODUCTION

Vicious Circle relates to the depression and anxiety in life along with my daily struggles with Crohn's and Colitis Disease, Bipolar and getting back into the dating scene. We all go through depression in different stages of our lives, whether it is our health, in the loss of a close one, or a loss of a job, or an ending to a marriage, or even just being rejected in the dating scene.

Depression is an illness, an illness that can and sometimes totally consumes your life. Most do not understand the affects that depression can have on some one's life. When you are depressed and anxious, you tend to keep all of your worries and fears alive. Depression and Anxiety can totally interfere with your life, in your social life, business obligations, taking care of your children, and also in my case, my marriage.

I never thought that I would see the day when I would be alone again; after living the last thirty one years with one man. The man that I thought I would be spending the rest of my life with until the day that I died. Here I am though, so depressed and all alone in this big world with no man to give my heart and soul too. Life does go on though, and there are just so many changes happening in my life now every day.

Margie Garrett

This is a book about my life, both during and after my divorce was final showing my depression and anxious thoughts as well as how I deal with my daily life with Crohn's Disease. Some of the experiences have been not only rewarding, but enlightening and then there are other experiences that have been, to say the least, ultimately dangerous. I have definitely learned a lot about myself through the last couple of years though. I hope that you can relate to some or all of my feelings of Depression, Anxiety and Hope for a brighter future.

I will be donating 10 percent of my profits for the sale of this book to help with Crohns and Colitis Disease and Depression organizations.

CHAPTER 1

Leaving My Home

As I leave the only life that I have known for thirty one years, I now have to face being single again. Not so easy when you are fifty one years of age. I have to face so many realities out here. Some good and some are very bad. I am now just living one day at a time; because the reality is that none of us really knows what tomorrow will bring, as my life has now proven.

Leaving home was so hard for me. Especially dealing with all of the uncertainties of not knowing where to go or how and if I could even make it on my own. I now needed to be dependent solely on myself. I stayed with our son for the first couple of weeks, and then moved from hotel to hotel until finally settling into a furnished apartment for the next few months. Saving all the money I could to purchase a mobile home, which by the way was about three hundred dollars that is right, it was only three hundred dollars. That was all that I could afford at the time. I knew I couldn't afford the apartment anymore, it was just too expensive, and it was just temporary anyways. The mobile home that I had purchased was horrible, absolutely horrible. It had black mold on the ceiling and down the walls in the living room, and the carpet was nasty and it need to be destroyed. It was all that I could afford though at the time, and was at the very least, a roof over my head.

Margie Garrett

After living there for a week or so, and working to remove the carpet and lay down the tile, I was so tired. Wanting to make this place a little more presentable and comfortable, but it was so hard. It was in such bad shape. Then, of all things, the furnace and the hot water heater went out and were no longer working. So for the next six weeks or so, in the middle of the winter, I was now forced to face the reality of no heat and very cold showers every day. Just think about that one for a minute. I know, in the summer when it is so hot, a nice cold or cool shower feels great. In the winter though, that is a different story, when you are already cold anyway. Topped off with no heat at all and being forced to take cold showers and have no heat to warm up afterwards.

It was so hard to force myself to do it every day, but I had to. It took me about two hours every day, when it would normally be a half an hour because of the cold water literally hurt my scalp and body. When I finally would be done, I had to just bundle up with a heavy robe and blankets over me and sit right in front of a space heater to try and get warm again. I made it through the winter though.

It is spring finally and it is a nice spring day I went to open a window to let some of the fresh air in, only to find out that the windows were not opening now. I have to now face the spring and summer months with no air conditioning and windows that would not open.

Not only am I hot, but you combine the heat and the black mold to the way I was feeling. So how do you think I am feeling like now? I felt like I was going to suffocate in there; and the mold and heat combined made me sick. Needless to say, I was outside more than I was inside. I dreaded going back in there every day, but once again, thought to myself that at the very least it is a roof over my head and I will just have to deal with it.

So here I am again heading toward the cold winter months; and facing the fact that I still have no furnace that works, windows that don't open and the black mold is getter worse every day. I, once again, decided that it was time to move again in hopes that just maybe this would be my last move.

Margie Garrett

I happened to find myself a little house on a lake, summer was pretty much over with by the time I found it. So when I had moved in there really wasn't time for any kind of fun on the lake. I really like it here though, was really a pretty area. So I did sign the one year lease and moved into it at the end of the summer. Everything seemed great. I was so happy with the house and the area. Then one day I went to take a shower and the water came out of the faucet all brown and rusty. It took him over a week to come out and then when he finally did, instead of fixing the problem, he ran a hose from my neighbors well to my house, and didn't even ask him and never fixed the problem. That went on for weeks, having to go take my showers elsewhere and being forced to buy bottled water for my cleaning and cooking. Once again, I dealt with it as best as I could.

Going through all of the changes, financial struggles and moves were bad enough; but then top all of that off with all the stresses that anyone of us that has gone through a divorce would have. Sure wasn't very easy for me dealing with all of this. Ending my marriage and going through the divorce was hard enough, but to deal with all of this too. I thought I was seriously going to lose my mind. I was just so stressed out all of the time. Wondering if my life was ever going to settle down and I could see some light at the end of the tunnel. Don't get me wrong, I knew at the very beginning when I left that things were not going to be easy for me, and I am okay with that.

For months after leaving my marriage, all I did was wonder where and how things in our marriage went so wrong. I would lay and think about how or what I could have done differently to make our marriage work, but I don't believe that I could have done anything more than I had done. It just didn't work; the love in our marriage was lost somewhere along the years.

I couldn't eat without getting sick, and I cried myself to sleep every night for what seemed like forever. I knew that the love was gone and the marriage was over, but still couldn't get past the pain of leaving the only life that I had ever known.

I know that leaving hurt my children, and for them, I am truly sorry. It really was the last thing that I ever wanted to do. However, at the end when I had left, they were all old enough at that point to accept it. I held the family together as long as I could until I just couldn't live like that anymore.

I felt very depressed and felt completely alone. Don't get me wrong, my children gave me a lot of support, and I am grateful to all of them for that. Let's face it though, when you no longer have your lover or someone there to talk to every day, the world outside seems so big, and you tend to get pretty lonely. The house is very quiet and the bed seems so big now when you don't have a man to share it with. So I would end up laying there crying myself to sleep every night.

Tunnel of Light

By Margie Garrett

As I cry myself to sleep at night
I wonder when I will see the light
seems so dark and out of sight
will I ever see the light.

Darkness and pain seem such a fight
I seem to have lost the light
I struggle and struggle every night
To try and find my lost light

Life does seem like such a fight
When you can never see the light
How will I ever find my light
With my freedom I might
If I don't cry every night

My space now is no longer tight
I can now find my bright light
I now have happiness in sight
I have now found my tunnel of light.

I for what seemed to be forever, seemed so all alone and scared of never being able to experience true love in my life again. All I know is that life does go on after divorce. There has to be a reason why this has happened to me. Why? I don't know. I just know that now I need to live my life the way that I was meant to live it. Maybe all of this was to experience all the trials and tribulations that go along with divorce to help others. I guess I have sure gone through enough, that I can actually say that I have walked in others footsteps.

I do know one thing though, and that is that I now need to make some changes in my life if I want things to get better. My life has definitely had a lot of ups and downs in it. All I do know is that I need to work on myself, to regain my self-worth, self-respect and self-confidence back if I am going to get any better. I just feel like I have completely lost myself and don't even know who I am anymore or what my purpose in life is. It is going to take me a long time to not only find myself, but figure out what that purpose is.

All of my life, from early childhood until now has been a struggle. I have felt like I can never do anything right. I fight to get from one day to the next. I have learned as a child, to just live and learn from all of my experiences though. Which is really all that any of us can do? Isn't it? Life is full of struggles. I will slowly, but surely rise above all of these struggles though, because I am very determined to get through all of this and find happiness; whether happiness is in my accomplishments or in finding that very special man.

At this point in my life; I am not really looking for a man. I just want to live again. Feeling so sheltered from the outside world for so long, I had a lot to learn; not only about me, but everything outside too. Right now, I just want to be able to just get through all of the divorce issues so that I can finally move forward in my life. All of this is enough stress to deal with.

Margie Garrett

All of the struggles that I have to go through already with all of the moving around and never really settling down into one place that I could actually call home were just too overwhelming for me. Never knowing where I would be from one day to the next. I really don't know, financially, whether I would be able to afford the place I am living in; depending now, solely on myself and a fixed income. I knew I had to budget myself. All of these emotions that are going on with me just seem to be so out of control. It has gotten to the point now, where I just feel like I don't really care about anything anymore. I know that I shouldn't be feeling this way, after all, it was my decision to leave. I do though. I just can't help how I feel. Sometimes, I just want to end it all. That is how depressed and alone that I really feel.

The only reason that really keeps me from ending my life is my children. I can't do that to them. If it wasn't for them though, I am not sure what I would do. I wasn't happy in the marriage and I am not happy now either. Life is just too hard these days. It has gotten to the point now where I am sleeping more and more every day. So depressed and withdrawn from living. Not really having anyone to turn to for help; because I knew that none of them could possibly understand why I had left my marriage for whatever reason that they may have had. They just thought I was crazy and didn't seem to believe a word that I said.

I basically gave up on getting any kind of support there. It just was never going to happen. So now you can see why I feel so all alone. I had hoped that they would always be there for me. Little did I know that they wouldn't be? Guess you really do eventually figure out who your true friends are in life, especially when something like this happens. Some made me feel like some kind of villain.

People, friends and family only see what they want to see and have really no idea what happens behind those closed doors, and some of them really don't care either. They sure don't want to hear about all of the problems. Where do I go to get some help and support? My children have always been there for me. I love them for that. However, I can't put all of my emotional feelings on them, they have enough of their own to deal with, knowing that the family is now broken and will never be the same again. That is a lot for them to deal with themselves. I just can't do that to them or anyone else for that matter.

Margie Garrett

I am just such an emotional wreck right now. It seems like all I do these days is sleep, cry and stare off into space like there is no tomorrow. I don't even feel like a human being anymore, instead I feel like I am nothing more than a zombie, just walking around aimlessly in a world I really don't want to be a part of anymore; a world full of anger, bitterness, fear and loneliness. I just can't seem to shake how I am feeling and get past all of the pain.

All of the emotional scars are so deep and so embedded. And bringing all of them to the surface seems so out of reach. It is just so hard dealing with all of the emotional scars. I don't honestly think that they will ever go away. I try so hard every day to move on and leave all of them in the past, but I just can't. Every day it just seems like more and more of them find their way back to the surface, and I am right back to the beginning again. Such a never ending battle it seems.

Every day is such a challenge getting through it. All I know is that I have to keep trying to, even if I get tired and just don't care anymore. The depression just seems to be getting stronger every day. And with no one to talk to about all of this, I get these feelings of suicide more and more. These days are so long and full of so many uncertainties. It has become more and more clear to me, that I am not going to be able to work through all of these emotions that I have. I knew that I needed to get some help or I was going to completely lose my sanity, and I sure didn't want that to happen. My life is such a mess. I don't like who I have become, always so full of anger and bitterness. I can't even remember who I am or what I was like before leaving home. That part of me was even left in the past and forgotten.

My health is getting bad again because of all the stress and everything that I have to go through, having been diagnosed with Crohn's Disease long before I left. You add all of the stress and depression to the already bad medical condition, and you can just imagine how bad I am getting. I have virtually no appetite as it is. So when I do eat, I feel like I am just forcing myself to. Then I can't even hold the food. It either makes me sick to the point of vomiting, or I end up with severe pain, or I have diarrhea for days at a time. So now on top of everything else, I have become dehydrated again and need to go in for my IV feedings in the hospital or clinic.

Margie Garrett

All of this, I wish would just go away, but it will never leave me. It is part of my life and has been for years now. I, like everything else going on, just have to deal with it as well. Just gets so hard and so overwhelming at times. Sometimes now, and more often than not, I just don't even want to get out of the bed and face everything. Right now I don't even feel like I am living, but instead just existing. I have to keep pushing myself more and more every day. I try so hard to just keep telling myself that things will eventually get better for me. It is just so hard though to be positive when everything in my life seems to be so negative all of the time. Never knowing from one day to the next what else is going to happen to pull me down.

Will my life ever get better, or is it always going to be this way? I don't want to live, because as far as I am concerned, this really isn't living. I just want to end all of the pain, suffering, and depression. Sometimes, when I go to bed at night, I think thoughts of just dying in my sleep in hopes that I don't have to wake up and face all of this over and over again, but it doesn't happen. I sure wish it would though. I can't help the way I am feeling anymore. I am just so tired of the fight of living and existing from day to day. I know I am wrong for feeling this way; I just can't help it though.

The suicidal thoughts are just getting stronger every day when there is so much negativity in my life. There is just not a lot of strength left in me anymore to continue fighting how I am feeling. I don't know if or when I will ever get past all of these feeling of knowing that I am alone again after living half of my life with one man and now this is my life. I just feel so out of it all of the time. I can't stand the way that I feel.

It has been weeks of fighting the landlord to fix the water well problem too, waiting and wondering whether that problem will ever be taken care of. Will all of the fighting ever end? Will things ever get better for me? Or is this the way I am going to have to live the rest of my life now? I am constantly battling with everything including my own feeling of pain, sadness, fear, anger, hopelessness, and worthlessness. Talk about depression. I can't take any of this anymore. I absolutely hate living right now. I don't know how much more I can take. I am really starting to feel like I am going insane. I thought I had found the tunnel of light when I left home, but I still feel like I am living in darkness. Will this ever end?

Darkness And Pain

My life is so full of darkness
Seems to be so pointless
All I see is blindness
As I am feeling oh so brainless

Have no feelings of boldness
Certainly see no brightness
My life is full of darkness
Feeling oh so breathless

My life so full of pain
Will I ever see light again
How can I explain
When I feel just so insane

Do I have a brain
No, all I am feeling, is drain
How can I explain
My life with all this pain

Will I ever be alright
Or ever find my light
Maybe if I stop the fight
I will try to stop tonight

Going to find some help I might
To finally get some insight
On how to stop my fight
And hopefully see my bright light

No more fight of darkness and pain
I need to find my life again
Only with help I will regain
A life with no darkness and pain.

CHAPTER 2

Getting Some Help

After so many months after leaving; and so many feelings of loneliness, depression and a lot of suicidal thoughts, I thought it would be best to get some help. I finally made the decision to see a Psychiatrist, because I knew that things that I was feeling and all of the emotions were just getting to out of control to deal with on my own. I needed some help dealing with all of this. I knew that I wasn't going to get any better, because all of these feelings were just getting worse. And since I was still covered under his insurance, I thought that I better, because I didn't know how much longer I would have the insurance or more importantly how much longer I could hold on, and so I had made an appointment with a Psychiatrist. I wasn't sure whether it would help or not, but it certainly couldn't hurt to go talk to someone. Just not ever talking to a Psychiatrist before, I didn't really know what would happen or how I would react. All I knew was that I needed to try.

And so I went in for my first appointment which was a couple of days later. It was a female thank goodness. So at least I felt a little bit more at ease. All that happened on my first visit was a lot of questions about my health and a lot of paperwork.

We didn't really talk about much else the first visit. I think she just wanted me to become comfortable with her so that eventually I could open up and let it all come out. I was as nervous as it was, so I was glad she didn't get into anything that day. She did tell me though that she felt that I was really troubled and that I should probably come in and talk to her at the very least twice a week for a while. She could see and hear a lot of depression in my eyes and in my voice. She had set my appointments up for Monday and Wednesdays every week, and I will have to go back and see her again in a couple of days.

Margie Garrett

My thoughts, right now, are just going in every direction. I can't seem to hold my concentration on anything right now. What do I do next? I am telling myself. Trying to get a grip on anything is so hard when your concentration isn't there anymore. Even though I didn't really talk to the Psychiatrist much about how or why I am feeling this way, I still feel so drained. I have absolutely no energy to do anything right now. So I just went and lay down for a while in hopes that I would feel better.

That didn't help though either. It only took my mind off of all of this for a couple of hours. I am just so tired of fighting what always seems to be such a losing battle. Will this ever end? I keep asking myself. Not ever being able to answer my own questions. How or why I continue sometimes, I really don't have a clue. Except for the fact that I am a very strong lady and that I have my children to think about. And I love them more than life itself. Thinking about what it would do to them if I just ended all of this. I just can't do that to them.

Living my life right now is so hard every single day. Not knowing from one day to the next, what other problems are going to come up, and how I will be able to deal with them. Sometimes, actually more times than not, my life just doesn't seem worth living anymore. I know that I need to keep the fight going though, if I am ever going to find my light at the end of the tunnel and be happy once again. Just seems so out of reach.

It is amazing finding out how much strength I have when I have had to endure so much in my life. My inner strength is really strong, and yet so weak at the same time. How can that be? How can I be so strong when I am feeling so weak all of the time? Always so hard fighting to pull on my inner strength to fight what always seems to be way too much for anyone to deal with. I just never know how I am going to deal with the next problem that arises.

I have one challenge after another and the decisions that I have to make too. Going to bed is hard enough for me and yet facing another day is something I just don't want to do anymore. The reality though is that if I ever want to see that light and not live in darkness, I really don't have any other choice. I have to do it, regardless of how hard it is for me. Otherwise, life will never be worth living.

Margie Garrett

Feeling so alone all of the time is so hard too. I seriously have absolutely no one that I can really turn to for support other than my Psychiatrist now. Never really having any true friends to speak of is really sad. This last year has felt like a lifetime. To be honest, I have no idea how in the world I have made it this long, but I did. Still to this day though, and by myself, still feel like I am just existing and not really living my life the way that I should be living it.

Will I ever get past all of this? I sure hope that I do. I do know that there has to be a better life for me out here. I just can't seem to find my life yet. I, sometimes, feel like I just don't care whether I do or don't anymore. That is just how seriously depressed that I am now all of the time. Most of the time, I just sit and stare off into space like there really is no tomorrow, because I just don't care whether tomorrow comes or not. What for? I tell myself, when every day feels the same way. I have nothing but pain and heartache. Still seems like nothing in my life is changing. Oh, wait a minute; it is changing alright, for the worse. I just keep getting more withdrawn from day to day, with every breath that I take.

A couple more days have gone by now, and my landlord still has not fixed the water well problem. I am getting so tired of having to go take my showers elsewhere, or buying bottled water to cook and clean the dishes with. So once again; I tried calling and speaking to him. Of course, as usual, he doesn't answer his phone or return my phone call. I have lived here only a couple of months, but had signed a one year lease with this guy.

He seems to be completely ignoring me and the whole situation with the well water problems that I have been having. He is in breach of his own contract. What in the world is the matter with him anyways? How long does he expect me to live like this? I don't think he really cares one way or the other.

I know one thing, I am not going to deal with all of this much longer, so he better do something to fix the problem and soon. If I have to fight him on this, I will take him to court. It is hard enough for me to try and deal with all of my feelings of worthlessness as it is. So I just don't need any more added and totally unnecessary stress in my life. I am paying him enough rent every month that I should have never had to be dealing with all of this.

Margie Garrett

Another day has gone by, and still no returned phone call from the landlord. Do I call him again and leave a message or do I just not pay him the rent for this month, which is now due? That will surely get his attention, when he doesn't receive his nine hundred dollars this month, of which he will not be getting the full amount anyways. I am now going to tell him that he now needs to adjust the payment to reflect the no use of water for the month. I am sure he won't be too happy about that one, but oh well; he will have to deal with it. I am just not going to pay for something that I haven't had in weeks. Shame on him!

I guess he feels like he can just get away with it because he is an attorney. Well he can think again, because the truth of the matter is, that he is not above the law by any means. He has to follow the same laws as everyone else, and I fully intend to prove it to him if he fights me on any of this. I just refuse to be treated this way by anyone. Being forced to live this way, he will be lucky if I don't sue him.

Well I gave him another chance, just the way that I am, yeah crazy I know. I left another message only to not receive a phone call back as I thought would happen. I was hoping he would though, but he didn't. Instead he just ignored it once again. So now I just deal with it and wait. The rent is due in a couple of days. When he doesn't receive it in the mail, he is going to have to call me if he wants his money. And believe me, when I say, he will get the same treatment back. As the old saying goes "what goes around comes around." Yes, you got that right if you thought that I am going to now ignore his phone calls to me. Maybe, he will now realize who he is dealing with in the future, and not try and screw me over.

For days now, he would leave messages for me to contact him. He even came over to the house, and I didn't answer the door. My vehicle was there, so he didn't come in though. Then he started sending me certified letters saying that I needed to contact his office about the overdue rent, which at this point, was a couple of days overdue. So I let him sweat it out a little longer to let him see what it is like to be screwed over. I figured when it started hurting him financially, maybe then he would take care of the problem.

Margie Garrett

Well, it is time to go see my Psychiatrist for the second visit. This one was more of a meet and greets kind of visit. She was still trying to get me to feel comfortable with talking to her, basically just talking about things going on in the world. And a little bit about my childhood, my siblings, and family life. She could tell that I was still very nervous and apprehensive. So, I guess, she didn't really want to push me into talking a lot about the way that I am feeling yet.

Just talking all the little talk though, made me tired once again. I seems like I get so tired so fast these days. Just dealing with all of the little every day chores is about all that I seem to be able to handle. When you add to all of them, I feel like I just want to crawl up in a big hole and let it all go. Not wanting to deal with anything else. I just wonder when she is really going to start talking to me about what is really bothering me. Although, once again, was grateful she hasn't started yet. The truth of the matter is, I just don't feel like I am ready to open up to anyone yet. I know that opening up all of the wounds is going to be so hard, and I really don't know how I will be able to.

I have always been one to hold all of my thoughts and emotions inside. Sheltering them away for anyone to see how I am really feeling. That has just always been the way for me, not really letting anyone in, which has been the way I have lived in order to survive the way I have felt about myself for so long in my life. I wanted everyone to only see me as a happy and a very strong and caring person, and not the unhappy and very weak person that I have become. I haven't felt good about myself in a very long time now. I hate the way that I feel about myself. Not wanting to feel weak anymore. I need to find myself and my strength again. I sure hope that I can.

All I can do every day now is to just keep trying, it is so hard though. Just waking up every morning is a struggle when you just wish you would have died in your sleep so you don't have to deal with anything anymore. Unfortunately, that is how I am feeling all of the time. I just have the attitude where I don't care or want to deal with any of it anymore. I keep going though, I have to. I push myself every single day, in hopes that the next day, will be a better one. I am just so tired.

Margie Garrett

I feel like my life right now consists of nothing more than crying, sleeping, fighting all my feelings alone or staring off into space. Not much of a life is it? These feelings I have had for so long in my life that I can't even love myself anymore, because I feel like I don't even know who I am or why I am even still here living this life. As far as I am concerned, it is and has been a life full of struggles. Do I really want to live anymore? I am so confused, on one hand I do and on the other hand I don't. I know only one thing for sure at this point, and that is that I have become someone that I definitely do not know, and definitely would have never wanted to know or love.

I sure hope that my Psychiatrist can help me find my way back to the caring and loving person that I once was, because I can't even remember who that person was or what I was like. I just feel so empty inside, like I have no love to give. I just want to be left alone, not wanting anyone to see the absolutely horrible unloving side of me. All of these horrible emotions that I have just keep coming out more and more every day.

So, as I lay here once again, feeling all of the angry thoughts, I cry myself to sleep hoping I won't wake up again. It didn't happen again though. Why am I still here on this Earth? Why do I feel like I am being punished every day by living this Hell? Is there a reason for this? I really still have no idea; I just wish that my life would end. Why won't it just end? Please let it end. I keep telling myself. I still feel like I am living in darkness and this is no way to live. Where is my light? Will I ever see it again?

Oh how I hate myself right now. I just need to stop feeling this way, and look at and remember all of the good things that have happened that have brought happiness to my life. My three beautiful children have brought so much happiness to me. I love them so much. They really are the one thing that keeps me going and at least trying to move on with my life.

I knew that leaving home was not going to be easy as I had said before; I guess I just didn't realize how hard it would really be. I still just can't believe it though. I keep asking myself if I am ever going to be able to get past all of these feelings and still can't give myself any answers. The only person I really talk to is my Psychiatrist. And I haven't even really started talking to her yet.

As weird as this may seem, because of what I had said before about not being ready to open up, I sure hope that the next visit she really starts getting me to talk more about everything. Maybe, opening up all of the wounds will somehow help me to start living again. I know I need to, not only for my own sanity, but for the kids' sake. Because I am sure that I am probably driving all of them nuts with all of my constant whining, moaning and groaning about everything that has happened to me. After all, these were all choices that I have made. I could have just stayed and not left home at all. So I need to deal with my choice and quit whining about how I am feeling now.

Well another day has come and gone, still waiting for the well water problem to be fixed and just dealing with the whole situation as best as I can. If he thinks for one minute that I am going to give in though, he better think again. That is for sure. I have no intentions, nor am I going to call him either.

I was actually hoping that the landlord would file a motion with the court for me to pay the rent or vacate the premises. He, I think, probably knows what I would do though. To be honest, he could be in serious trouble for forcing me to live in an extremely unhealthy home. He would be in trouble with the Health Department and he is also in breach of his own contract. That is why I am just dealing with it and sweating it out so he realizes that I am not going to pay all of the rent, nor am I going to pay him anything until the problem is fixed completely.

It is Monday again, time for my third visit with the Psychiatrist. So I apprehensively went to see her, not knowing again what would happen. This visit fortunately or unfortunately, whichever the case may be. She did get into more of how I am. It was mostly just through the questionnaire that she wanted me to fill out, that would give her an idea of what has been going on in my life and why I am feeling the way that I am.

She asked me a few more questions that weren't on there. And in answering a couple of really hard ones, I broke down and started to cry. I could barely even talk to her. I was such an emotional wreck. She had decided to ask a few more. This visit was so much harder than the first couple. She said that she could tell that I am deeply depressed and that my emotions are all over the place, and that I virtually have no concentration at all.

Ann, my Psychiatrist had now diagnosed me with severe depression and Bipolar. She put me on some medications to help me deal with my depression and suicidal thoughts. She also told me, that if the thoughts come back or become worse than they already are, that I call her right away for some help dealing with all of them. She also recommended me to write down my thoughts in a journal and to bring it to her for my next visit. These thoughts, she said, will help with the treatments. I sure hope that they help me. She also gave me something to help me sleep at night, as I always end up laying there with all of these thoughts and crying myself to sleep at night.

Margie Garrett

When I had left the office, I immediately went to get the prescriptions filled so I could get on them right away. Tonight, for a change, I sure hope that I fall right off to sleep. It says to take the pill about twenty minutes before going to bed. I am ready to go to sleep, so I did just that. Wow, about ten minutes after taking them, I am in the bed. She was right, when she told me that I should fall right off to sleep, because I sure did. I think for the first time in a very long time, I may actually fall asleep without all of the crying.

I slept so hard and for so long last night that I just couldn't believe it. It shouldn't have shocked me though feeling as exhausted as I had been for so long. Once the other medications for the depression start working, I am not really sure what to think. Sometimes, I feel like I am just staring off into space, I know that I have said that before, but it is true. I am not a zombie, but at the same time, I am alive, but really alive and not living if that makes any sense at all. I just feel like I am no more than just existing. Everyone tells me that it is going to take some time for the medications to work. So I just need to be patient and wait and see how all of them are really going to affect me.

Now with all of these added medications to the ones that I am already taking for the Crohns Disease, I feel like I have a pharmaceutical here. It feels like I am taking medication all day long now and am even more tired than I already have been. Feeling like I can hardly function at all to do some of the littlest things. Now I am always trying to remember what pills I have taken and which ones I haven't taken yet, and not forgetting to take any of the doses for any of them. Talk about hard, you bet it is.

I am now taking about seven different prescriptions for the Crohns Disease, Bipolar, Severe Depression, and for sleeping at night. This in itself is so exhausting. I know that every single one of them is important and that I need to make sure to remember every dose of every one of them. I am managing so far though, and I know that I have to keep up with them; otherwise they won't help me at all.

For the first few days on the new medications, I had a lot of side effects such as, dizziness, lightheadedness, diarrhea, vomiting, and drowsiness. I also had some pretty bad headaches. Like everything else, I dealt with all of it and waited it out in hopes that they would all subside. For the most part, most all of them that were on a daily basis, did. Or at least I no longer had them every day and all day long. I still had to deal with all of the pain, vomiting and diarrhea that I virtually have all of the time, but at least the other symptoms had gone away. The medications do seem to be helping me.

Margie Garrett

I am not feeling like I want to end my life, but rather just start trying to live it again. I am still by far not ready to go out to any clubs or meeting any new people yet. So, instead, I had purchased internet service. I thought I would just go online and check out different sites and maybe work on some genealogy, which I always found very interesting. I figured with the internet, genealogy and some games I would possibly be able to get my mind off of everything else for a while. It is working too, but I am still feeling so alone and bored with my life. I know that all of this is just going to take time to get through. I am just a very impatient lady these days.

Trying to build back my self-confidence and self-respect and learning to love myself again is just not such an easy task for me, especially, when I am feeling all of the guilt of breaking up my family. I tried so hard and for so long to keep us all together, really I did. I am just so sorry that I couldn't do it any longer. I just couldn't. I can only hope that someday my children will understand why I felt the way that I did in not really having any other choice. I just don't want to be unhappy anymore.

I think, with the help of the new medications, that I am finally getting past all of the suicidal thoughts. Now I just keep telling myself that I deserve to be happy. Ann, my Psychiatrist, has helped me a lot already, but I still have such a long road ahead of me with all of my emotions. How long is it going to take? I have absolutely no idea. I just know that I have to keep trying. Just taking one day at a time and learning to live all over again, seems so impossible sometimes. What other choice do I really have, except to live from day to day now?

Not knowing how I will handle every day is the hard part. Anyone can wake up every morning and just live in existence. I just keep telling myself that this is not the kind of life I want to live. I want to love and be loved. Why is it so hard to find? I have absolutely no idea. Just seems to me, that a lot of people look out only for themselves. I could be that way too. I don't want to live my life that way though, nor do I ever think that I was that way. If there is one thing that I do remember, that is that I always seemed to help others that needed the help, and I had always put my family before myself. That is just the way that I have always been and that is one quality in my life that I don't ever want to change. That is very important to me.

Margie Garrett

Maybe, that is what I was put on this earth for was to help people in need. I know that there are so many men, woman and children who have been abused in their lives, and so many couples who have gone through a very bad divorce. Then there are also the ill, homeless and the poor. There are so many people that are in need of some form of help. I know that I am not a Counselor or a Psychiatrist, but let's face it; you don't have to have the credentials to be able to help everyone out there. I am not by any means, saying that we shouldn't seek the help of professionals because I have had to myself.

Everyone can always use the help and support of others at times. Whether it is a helping hand or someone to talk to when things seem to become so overwhelming that you don't think you can handle it anymore. Maybe this really is what I need to consider doing with my life. I think that not only will my helping others help them, but it will help me to regain my self-confidence and self-esteem. Well at least that will give me something to think about. Sure is something that I probably would really like to do in my life. That would be something that would definitely give meaning to my life.

I have been through an awful lot of challenges in my life time; that I can honestly say that I have probably walked in others footsteps. I am sure that I can at least be a source of support for others if, absolutely nothing else. I still need to work on myself first and make me love myself and become a much stronger woman. I am sure that I will, it is just taking me longer than I expected it too. I guess I didn't realize how unhappy I really was until now. Once I get through all of my own emotions and can deal with every day life's struggles again, then and only then, will I be able to actually move ahead in my goals of helping others, which is seriously what I would love to do with the rest of my life.

Instead of constantly taunting myself with all of my feelings of inadequacies and all of the guilt, I just keep telling myself all of the time, I can do this. I will become a much stronger and more independent woman. Eventually, it will happen, and I will probably shock myself. I will though, that is how determined I am to make things in my life better. Life could be so much worse, so I think about all of the people out there really suffering. That truly is what keeps me up in spirit and motivated enough to move forward and to try new things in my life.

Margie Garrett

As I write all of these thoughts and ideas down in my journal, I remembered to take the journal to my next appointment with Ann, my Psychiatrist, yes I am still seeing her for advice, guidance, and help dealing with everything. She told me though, what I already knew, and that is that I still have a lot of my own issues to work through first. She is still concerned that I have not been dealing with all of my thoughts of ending my life because of all of the emotions that I still seem to have. She asked a lot more questions that were pretty hard to answer this visit. I just didn't know how to answer some of them.

And then, the oh so obvious question was, "Why do you want to end your life?"

"Why not, I don't really feel like fighting a losing battle anymore, so why should I fight it over and over again?"

"Because for one; you have your three beautiful children who love you very much. Don't you think that your committing suicide wouldn't hurt them? They would be devastated and I think that deep down inside, you know that."

"I know, but I can't help how I feel."

"Well you need to think about yourself and learn to love yourself and your life again."

"I know, but it is so hard all of the time."

After this session, and like the previous ones, I was once again thoroughly exhausted. As I sit on the sofa, after arriving back home, I nearly fell asleep. I am going to go lay down, I tell myself. I just can't do anything else right now. I fell asleep and awakened a couple of hours later. This afternoon nap of mine is becoming a regular habit lately, just because I am so tired. Still not sure whether being so tired is a cause of all of the stress in my life, or whether it is from all of the medications that I am now taking. Either way, when it gets to be afternoon, I am so ready to go lay down for at least a little while. With so much going on with me, it is hard to tell. I don't fight the naps though, actually I am grateful to have my mind off of everything and just rest.

I feel like the sessions with Ann are definitely helping me, as I feel the days seem to be getting easier and easier to deal with. There is less stress and I have been having some positive thoughts about my future instead of nothing but negative. When I first started seeing Ann, all that I had was nothing but negative thoughts. Slowly but surely, I am finally starting to see, at the very least, a glimpse of light.

Margie Garrett

Working with Ann has been a great comfort. Having a sounding board and someone to be there to hear me, and actually listen, really does help so much. At this point, I certainly need all the help and support that I can get. I am so glad that I actually feel comfortable enough to talk to her about anything including my deepest thoughts, which has always been so difficult for me to open up to anyone. She just seems to bring out everything I am feeling from deep down inside my heart and soul. It is amazing.

Every time I see her and talk about all of my feelings, I feel so much stronger. I know that I still have a long way to go though, but I am slowly getting there. At least I am feeling better about myself. I felt like sometimes I had just put myself in a cocoon for no one to ever see me or see what I am going through. I just never really wanted anyone to see that side of me. A side of me, that is just so weak and tired of fighting everything all of the time.

I finally, after a few days, contacted my landlord and told him

"I have no intentions of paying this months' rent until the water is fixed and I can actually use it without tapping into my neighbors well."

His answer to me was "If you don't pay, then I will see you in court."

I guess he figured because he is an attorney that he has the upper hand and that I would really have no choice but to pay the rent regardless of whether he fixes it or not. The problem is that he isn't dealing with an idiot who is going to idly stand by and take that from him.

I told him "You don't want to take me to court."

"Why is that?" He said.

I told him, "Because, if you do I will not hesitate to tell the judge that you have forced me to live in an unhealthy home and threatened this court hearing if I don't pay you. When and only when you fix my water completely, will you get the rent? You are in breach of your own contract and I will not take any more of your threats so fix it. This conversation is over. Good bye."

I didn't hear from him again for another several days. Still living in this unhealthy home, I had no other choice but to consider the possibility that I would have to move yet again. I feel like I am never going to be able to settle down into a home of my own.

CHAPTER 3

Finally Free

Well looks like my divorce hearing has finally been scheduled after over a year of leaving him. I really didn't think the day would ever arrive, that I would actually be free to start living. Though I have to wait about six weeks though, that day will finally be here. I am so nervous and sad on one hand and totally excited on the other. To know that in six weeks I will be free of my past and be able to move on with my life regardless of how scared I am, is encouraging. Now being afraid to start all over again as a fifty one year old, is just not that easy. And not knowing what my future really holds for me. Or will I be alone the rest of my life? After divorce, do any of us really know? No we don't, but we will be free of all the sadness, even though I feel rejected.

For me the next several weeks seemed like forever. Just counting the days, is what I am doing now. Having all kinds of mixed feelings, I now just wait for that day to come and I ask myself all of the time now, how will I feel? What will I do now? What is my purpose on this Earth? And I tell myself, I just don't know because somewhere along the way I lost myself. I don't remember who I am or what kind of person I use to be. I had put the walls up around me so high that no one could break them down. I just don't care anymore.

At this point in my life, I thought I would, more than likely, be alone for the rest of my life, a lonely old lady. All I could do is hope that someday I will find that very special man to fill the void that I seemed to have now. I have had a lot of memories both good and bad. How could I not have? I have three beautiful children and two granddaughters, so of course there are many happy memories too.

Will I ever find love again? I sure hope so. I long for a man to snuggle up with in front of a good movie, or to take walks with in the park. A man, whom I can truly love and have in my life that loves me, and accepts me for who I am and not what he would like me to be, whether, I ever find that man remains to be seen. I sure can dream though. Right? After all, they say that dreams can come true. Time will tell. As the day gets closer, I begin to get very depressed again along with being so scared. Seems like a life time ago that I was single.

Margie Garrett

A Different Life

I am free to live
And free to give
A different life I have to live
Full of promises and dreams
And no more screams

I have cried my tears
And have been full of fear
No more fear though
As I have a different life to live

I have just lived in existence for all of those years
My life now full of anger and fear
No longer do I have the anger and fear
As I have a different life to live

And now I have so much to give
A heart of gold for all to see
So now let me be me
I have finally found peace and happiness for me

Even to this day, about a year after I left, I still cry myself to sleep at night. I loved him so much. Why do I feel that he didn't love me? Why? I ask myself that question all of the time. I doubt myself, wondering if it was something that I had been doing or not doing. Was it the way I look? I have absolutely no idea. I wish that I did. Maybe, than it would have helped me to understand. The not knowing why, I think, is the worst part for me?

Every night as I lay in the bed, all of these thoughts seem to be racing through my mind. It just seems endless in trying to find the answers. I just feel so hopeless all of the time, crying myself to sleep every night and only getting a couple of hours of sleep just isn't helping me to cope with any of these feelings. I am filled with feelings of hopelessness, helplessness, anger, fear, sadness and bitterness. Right now I don't like the way that I am feeling at all. I know I have so many changes in my life to cope with, and I just don't know if I can do it.

Margie Garrett

Every day I am questioning myself. I am literally every morning, sitting on the side of my bed reassuring myself that I can do this and that I will be all right. It is so hard though trying every day to convince myself. Where is that strong woman I use to be? Where did she go? Will I ever find her again? Or is she lost forever? I just don't know anymore. To be honest, the sadness, fear and hatred seem to be consuming me. I sure don't like what I have become, but right now I just can't help how I am feeling every day. I wish that my marriage would have lasted, because I loved him so much that it hurts this badly.

All I can do now is live from day to day. I am just trying hard to deal with everything going on in my life and my feelings. I know that it is going to take a lot of work on myself to find myself the way I was long ago, but more importantly, learning to love myself and who I am. I think that is going to be the hardest. I have to keep trying though. If I don't love myself, the truth is, how can anyone really love me? I have to find that strong, caring, happy and giving person that I believe I use to be.

There is so much living I want to do, so many places I always wanted to go, and yet at this point I really don't care anymore. It just doesn't seem important to me at all. I have lost all of my hopes and dreams. I guess some or all of those are lost forever, at least some of them are. Hopefully, in time, I will have some new dreams. I can only hope for a brighter future.

I continue to see Ann and get the help that I desperately need to cope with all of this. She has been someone that I can really count on to talk to. Without her, I don't know how I would have made it this far. The preparation for the divorce, the three attorneys I had to deal with as well as the arbitrator seems to be so overwhelming. I thought so many times I was just going to just lose it. Ann helped me through all of it though.

I am so full of so many mixed feelings these days. I can't eat without getting sick. I can't sleep or go lay down even, without crying, because I just can't stop thinking about all of this. Every day just seems harder for me than the day before. I thought that it would get easier, but it is not. One day I am up and the next day I am down. I always feel like I am taking three steps forward and then two back. It is a constant battle for me every day not knowing what will be thrown at me to have to deal with.

Margie Garrett

I am now down to the last week before the divorce is final. The mixed feelings are getting stronger and stronger every day. I am crying more and more now with so much sadness. When I give my heart and soul to one man for so many years of my life, and then one day all of the love is gone, it is so hard to explain how much I am hurting.

That week before the divorce hearing, I didn't want to talk to anyone or see anyone. I just wanted to be left alone. It was like losing my best friend and lover. I felt like my whole world was crashing down on me. The walls I put around me stayed up. Half of my life was gone now. I pretty much lay in the bed, thinking and crying all day and all night, to the point that my eyes hurt and I feel completely drained. Now I really didn't have any strength left in me. All I kept thinking was that I had nothing to live for. Like a big part of me died. I have a big void in my life now, and I really don't know if it will ever change, and to be honest, right now, I really don't care.

Well today is finally the day. As I go into the courtroom, I look at him and he looks at me. It was so hard for me going in there and realizing that this is it, and that it is truly over for us. There is no turning back now.

So now the divorce is final. I am free to live my life the way that I want to. To do what I want and when I want to without answering to anyone anymore. Now, for some reason, finalizing the divorce seems like the end. I really need to think about it as a beginning though. I feel so totally alone now.

CHAPTER 4

Living My Life

I try every day, to remember all of the good memories that we shared, as I try really hard to forget all of the bad ones. Unfortunately, I can't forget the bad ones, nor can I erase them from my memories. All I can do is try to think about the good ones, because we really did have them with our children growing up and with our son's daughters. All were good memories.

As I start a whole new beginning in my life, I never thought I would ever lose the support of longtime friends. I knew that I would be alone with not having him in my life anymore and the children all were grown up and out on their own, living their own lives as they should be.

I sure wish that my friends hadn't deserted me. I am so depressed now. I would have liked to have had someone to talk to, and a shoulder to cry on every once in a while, but I didn't. Yeah, I truly am alone.

What is the old saying that I have heard,
"For things to change, I had to change, and for things to get better, I had to get better".

There is also another one that I have to live by now and that one is,

"Things don't just happen, they happen for a reason".

I just keep repeating these two phrases to myself every day, because now I need to start loving myself, finding myself and living my life. It is just going to be really hard for me.

Mixing and mingling and talking to people that I don't know, is just so hard, as I am kind of a shy woman. What in the world am I going to do with the rest of my life? I guess for right now, I just need to work a lot on myself. So I just keep telling myself every time I become depressed and anxious and start crying, that this really isn't helping me. I just need to stop all of it. For some reason, I don't know, I just can't seem to though. I just can't shake all of the feelings.

Right now, I am living between my walls. They are so high. It is going to be so hard for anyone to get in. With the way that I am feeling right now, I sure don't want anyone to see me this way. I am such a mess. I just feel like I am drowning in my own sorrow. Depression and my anxieties are taking over my life. Kind of a pity party I guess you would call it. I just really don't care too much about anything or anyone.

I know that some are concerned and some just want to be nosy and find out what had really happened. If I truly thought that they cared and were sincere, I would have had no problem talking to them, but they weren't. So I didn't talk to any of them. The only one I would talk to and tell my inner most thoughts to was Ann, my Psychiatrist. Besides, she is the only one that can really help me through all of this and try and make some sense as to why any of this had happened to me.

Margie Garrett

As my therapy sessions continue with Ann, I realized that as much as I didn't want to admit it, a lot of the way that I had been and still am feeling was and still is my own fault. I allowed myself to become a victim to the loss of myself, and I just didn't care anymore. I have the attitude of why bother, instead of relying on my own strengths and keeping my head up and continuing to fight the battle. I was just too tired and gave up on myself. I let all of my depressions and anxieties come alive and just lived with it. I can't blame that on anyone but myself.

I now have to really fight to bring myself back to life, that loving, caring, considerate, passionate, person I use to be instead of this depressed, bitter, hurt and angry person that I am right now. This is definitely going to be a long and very rough road for me. I am determined though. It may take me years to find myself again, but I will. You will see.

Life does go on after divorce and all I can do is hope that at some point I will get over all of my anxious and depressed feelings and allow that one caring, loving, affectionate, man in my life that can start to break down my walls, one by one, that I have built up around me so high, and love me. I sure hope that is in my future. I can dream, I have to, it is what keeps me going. Although, at this point in my life; I can't imagine any man wanting to have anything to do with me. I can't really blame them either. Could you? Because to be quite frank, if the tables were turned, I sure wouldn't want to have anything to do with me either. At least not with the way I feel about myself and life for me as it is right now. I just have a very bad outlook on life.

I am very skeptical about everything and everyone. I can't seem to trust what anyone says or does for me right now. I have to be very honest; I have no trust or feelings for anyone right now, one way or the other. My depressions and anxieties just seem to be getting worse and worse every day now.

It is so sad, having to live with all of this doubt and fear every day. It is certainly going to take a lot of love for me to break down my walls. I don't want to be alone for the rest of my life either. I won't let another man take my heart and soul again for quite some time.

Margie Garrett

It is really going to be hard for the next man, if there is ever going to be one, to prove to me that he really does love me. It will be just as hard for me to recognize what true love really is. I have to let all of these thoughts go right now though, because I am not ready physically or emotionally to experience any of those feelings.

Working on myself, is what I need to be doing right now. I have so many mixed feelings and thoughts all of the time. Completely tired I am. All I can do for now is to just live one day at a time. Trying to do that is hard enough. I never realized how tiring it could be. Never knowing how I would get through one day, and never knowing what the next day would be like. Life for me is so unpredictable. I think the constant loneliness and uncertainties of anything in my life is really scary to me.

The loneliness is just consuming me with not going out anywhere, doing anything or really talking to anyone. I know that at some point I need to really start living again. I guess I am just not ready for the outside world yet. I feel safe and guarded from any added pain. I can't let my wall down, not even a crack for anyone to get in. Sheltering me just feels safe to me. I am lonely but safe. Am I wrong in doing this? I don't think so; I don't want anyone seeing me this way. It is just better this way for right now. I know eventually I will have to venture out, just not now.

Most of my days, I tend to just sit on my sofa with no television or radio, staring into space. Sitting there like a vegetable. I feel like I have been stabbed in the back and am completely numb. Talk about depressed, yes I am really depressed. I think, sometimes, that if I stay this way than no one can ever hurt me again. Do I really want to live like this though? Life is always a risk. Is taking risks really worth living? Maybe, but I don't really know anymore. I am just so afraid of being hurt or rejected, so for me taking risks is not what I really want to do.

I lost the love for myself so how can I ever love anyone else now? The truth is, if I don't love myself, then how can I really expect anyone to ever love me either? This is just all so hard for me emotionally and extremely tiring for me to deal with. So I just sit here on my sofa with absolutely no emotions at all. Living like nothing more than a zombie. I just don't know how to live or love anymore. I don't know what it will take or even how long it will take before I can step out of this major depression that I am in right now. Almost like I have completely suffocated myself into a cocoon, afraid of the fear of getting hurt or staying in it and hurting myself by not wanting to take the risk of living the life I was meant to live. Whatever, that may be. I know I was put on this Earth for a reason, I just don't know what it is yet. And I just need to keep searching for my place in this crazy world of ours.

Margie Garrett

I decided that maybe going on a 7 night cruise to the Eastern Caribbean with my daughter might be what I need right now to take my mind off of everything and just get away from it all. And so I asked her if she would go with me, and she agreed.

Tomorrow I am going to go online and check out some of the cruises and see what they have to offer. I want to plan the cruise in the spring, so that we can have a great start to a summer. Neither one of us has ever been on a cruise before, so this will be really nice for us to spend some quality time together. I need to spend time with her more than she knows. I love her so much, and I know that she has been through a lot lately too, not that my sons haven't been, because they have too. They just can't get away right now with work, and I did help them with homes.

As I wake up this morning, I get my cup of coffee of course, and then go online to check out the cruises available and what the prices are to go on a seven night cruise. I am thinking an Eastern Caribbean, because it would take us to the Bahamas, Cozumel, Belize and we would be leaving out of Miami, Florida.

At first, I thought about just driving from Michigan to Florida to catch the cruise ship, but by the time we would get to Florida, we would be so tired that we really wouldn't be able to enjoy much of the first day. Therefore, I also decided to check into air flights to Miami for us too. It would be worth the price to just fly out there rather than pay for all the gas, parking and time that it would take us to get there by car. Also, as far as the cruise goes, I am not even going to bother checking into what the inside cabins would cost, because if I am going to go on a cruise, we are going to want a balcony that we can breathe the fresh air of the ocean waters whenever we want to. We would not be able to do that at night when we are in the cabin if we get an inside one.

Margie Garrett

When I started planning the cruise, I forgot all about the fact, that I have absolutely no credit or credit card to do any of this. I felt so low, that I had to ask my daughter to use her credit card for the cruise and the air travel, when I had asked her if she wanted to go with me. I, of course, would give her the money for all of this, but still was very embarrassing to me to find myself this low. She, of course, said that she would, but I sure felt so horrible about it, because I had to ask her to do that for me. Well, the cruise and air travel are all paid for, and we will be going on the cruise in about four months.

These last four months went so quickly, and we are so excited about the cruise. We leave for the cruise now the day after tomorrow. I thought that maybe I better pick up some things for the cruise including some motion sickness pills just to be on the safe side. I don't know how we will be on the ship, so better safe than sorry. I certainly hope that we don't need to use them though.

I don't think that I have slept much at all the last couple of days, and I don't expect that I will be able to sleep tonight either, since we leave for the airport in the morning. I am going to pick her up around seven in the morning and our flight leaves Detroit around ten o'clock and we get into Miami around noon.

The flight went well and we arrived in Miami without too much of a delay. We were able to catch the bus transfer to the cruise ship. Wow, this is so amazing. I still can't believe that we are actually going on this cruise ship. I can't wait to board and see our cabin and everything that this cruise ship has onboard.

We boarded the cruise ship, went and found our cabin and just gazed out the balcony at the ocean waters. The first night was viewing ocean waters, having a couple of drinks and the great food that they had onboard. We just walked around and went on the deck and just laid back and relaxed with our drinks.

It seems like I, for once in a very long time, had not a care in the world. It was as though all of the stress, depression and anxiety from life in general had just been lifted off of me. I can only hope that the Crohn's and the pain stay under control too, so that I am not sick the entire cruise. I am good so far though, but than this is only the first day of the cruise too. Well, it is now time for us to head back to the cabin, we are both tired, been a long but very exciting day for us.

Margie Garrett

When we woke up the next morning, we just went out to our balcony for a few minutes and just sat and stared out at the ocean waters. So peaceful the waters seem. Then we went down for some breakfast and then just lay out on the deck again for a while.

Today we will be arriving in Belize. Yesterday we had purchase some of the excursions and one of them was to go snorkeling in the clear blue waters of Belize, which is supposed to be a great spot for snorkeling. And so that is what we will be doing later this afternoon.

We had decided not to board the boat to go into the city because of the danger, so we just took the other boat just into the waters for snorkeling only, and then went back to the cruise ship afterwards to wait for the others that took a chance and did go. The snorkeling was good, I had a little bit of a problem but I was able to get the snorkeling equipment to work after a while. The rest of the day and night were once again very relaxing with not a care in the world. We walked the ship, going for a drink here and there, or just went up to the deck.

We now have two days at Sea, where we just relax on deck sun tanning and listening to music or reading a book. My daughter used her time to relax, getting some suntan and reading Twilight. I am just feeling so relaxed and at ease for the first time in so long. We sure are not starving here on the ship, there is just so much food being served all of the time. If you are ever hungry it really isn't anyone's fault but your own.

Our next port is in Cozumel, where we will be going on a Dolphin Swim Excursion. We both love dolphins and are excited about the fact that we can actually get right down in the water with them. And so we did just that. The dolphins came right up to us and we were even actually able to get pictures of us kissing the dolphin. I just love dolphins and always have. I heard though that they are even more dangerous than sharks, somehow I find it hard to believe, but apparently they are extremely territorial.

The next day was spent at sea and then we reached the Bahamas, where we just went and did some sightseeing on the island. We had another great day there too, and taking lots of pictures.

Margie Garrett

Well this is our last night onboard the ship, we are now heading back across the waters to Miami and ending an absolutely awesome time on this cruise. I sure don't want it to end, but we both know that we will at one point take another cruise that is for sure. And so we enjoyed our last night on the ship and then went up to our cabin and sat out on the balcony for a while until we finally lay down and got some sleep.

I really didn't want to go back home. I wish that we could just stay on the cruise ship where I didn't have to deal with any of the troubles at home. I think, at least I hope, that my daughter enjoyed the cruise as much as I did. And so we are now home, and life as it was, was still waiting for us here. Nothing changed and all worries and problems are still here and have just been waiting for me to have to deal with. At least I had a week though, that I didn't have to deal with any of it; a week of so much enjoyment that will never be forgotten and will always be a part of me. I sure hope that I will be able to take another cruise sometime in the future. However, the reality is that I don't know if I will ever be able to afford another cruise, because of all of my debts that seem to just be burying me.

CHAPTER 5

Stepping Out

As I continue working on myself and the things that I need to change in my life, I am now stepping out of my own comfort zone. I would never get better unless I start to face reality. I can't stay there or things will never change for me. So more and more, I started to chat online in some of the different singles chat rooms, hoping to meet new people and make some new friends. With as shy and as uncomfortable as I am in mixing and mingling, I knew that I would have to do just that, push myself.

After checking out some of the singles sites, I had learned that there are singles parties at some of the local clubs in the area that I could go to and meet some of the men and women that I had been talking to online. Talk about scary; I have never done anything like this before. Therefore, I really had no idea what to expect when I got there or even if I would be brave enough to go in by myself. This is so hard. I was not going there for the dating scene right now, but instead, only to meet some of the others that are going through some of the same things that I am going through.

I mostly have been talking to females and getting to know them, and hopefully, can go to my first party with at least one of them. I just don't want to go into one of them by myself right now. Chicken? Yeah, I know. Oh well. I am trying hard to get out on my own. Talking to men, still makes me very nervous, never knowing how to take them or how to react to them.

The first party is coming up in about a month or so. I had been talking to Linda and Pat to see if they were going.

I asked, "Linda, are you going to the party next month?"

She responded, "I am really not sure whether I will be able to or not. I have a baby shower to go to that afternoon and I am not sure how late that is going to go. I am hoping that I can make it just not sure right now. Are you going?" I explained,

"I am not feeling very comfortable going by myself, and that is why I asked if you were. I think I will ask Pat if she is going to go."

Linda said, "I don't blame you, I know that when I first started going, I didn't want to walk into a party by myself either. I hope that she is going and that you two can go together."

"Thanks Linda, I hope you will be able to go", I responded.

"I really want to. Well I have to get to the store, so I will talk to you later. Bye for now."

"Bye Linda"

I went online and left a message for Pat asking for her phone number so that I could talk to her, and luckily she messaged me back giving it to me.

I, immediately, called her. "Hi Pat."

Pat answered, "Hi Margie, how are you doing?"

"I am okay. I was wondering if you were going to the next party. I hope so, please say yes. I really want to go, but I won't go by myself. I am just way to chicken," As I am laughing.

Pat says, "Sorry, I will not be able to make this party because I have a wedding to go to this time. Sorry."

I answered, "Oh, okay, I sure was hoping you would. Well I hope you have a great time at the wedding. Who is getting married?"

"My brother's daughter is that day. It ought to be a great reception. I can't wait. She will be one very beautiful bride. Oh sorry Margie got to go, I have another call coming in, but I will talk to you later okay. Bye for now."

"Bye Pat."

Personally I think that her brothers daughter is nuts, I don't know that I would ever get married again. The number of horrible men and woman definitely out way the good ones for sure. So over the next couple of weeks, I tried to talk to new people every day in hopes that it wouldn't be quite so hard.

I had been talking to this one guy online who lives in West Virginia, and we had been talking for quite a while now. He seems like a really nice guy. He was coming into town in the next couple of days. His name is John.

John had asked, "I am going to be in town on Friday, do you think we could meet somewhere for a drink?"

I said, "I would really like that."

I just realized that this is Wednesday, and we are meeting on Friday. Yikes!!

Well it is already Friday, how quickly the time had gone by. Will I be able to actually meet with John, or will I cancel the date because of being anxious and so nervous that I just can't do it? In anticipation of meeting with John, I called my beautician and made an appointment to have my hair and nails done. After all, first impressions are so important. I have to have someone else do it for me because in my married years, I rarely ever had my hair done and never had my nails done. Nor did I ever use any makeup either. So this is all so new to me.

I went to the mall to get a nice shirt to wear with my jeans. This just happened to be my very first date after my divorce. I am so nervous. All of the anxiety and nervousness is really coming out now. If nothing else happens, at least I, for once, looked pretty good. Different, that is for sure.

John had called me Thursday night and asked me, "So, Margie, are we still on for Friday?" "Yes, I am looking forward to meeting you tomorrow night John." "So where would be a good place to meet?" "There is a sports bar that we can meet at. The name of it is called Rogers'. It is in Warren. Would you like to meet there?" "Sure that is fine. I will be in town around five o'clock. Do you think that we could meet there around eight o'clock?" I said, "Eight o'clock would be great", he responded.

So, here I am, sitting in Rogers' waiting for John. My anxiety and nervousness was playing havoc on me. I can't believe that I am even doing this. Here I am though, sitting by myself in a sports bar, unbelievable. It was ten minutes before eight o'clock, and a guy walks in acting like he was looking for someone. He walks over to me and says, "Hi, are you Margie?" I replied, "Yes, Hi you must be John right?" "Yes I am. It is nice to finally meet you." "It is nice to finally meet you too John." What in the world did I get myself into here? I was so full of fear that I would totally fumble on my words and act like an absolute fool. I just tried to be myself though.

As the evening continued, it turned out to be a really nice date. Jon was everything that I had hoped for. Not only did he seem like a very caring and loving man, but a gentleman too. The evening was spent getting to know each other a little better. I wasn't sure where things could go with us, especially with him living so far away though.

John asked me, "So tell me Margie, what are your likes, dislikes and what are you looking for in a man?"

I replied, "Wow John, that is definitely a loaded question," As I laughed.

"Let's see if I can give you all of the answers that you are looking for. What are my likes? Well I like to go dancing, watch movies in or out of the home, swimming, boating, camping, canoeing, and snowmobiling, a walk in the park or on a beach, picnics and traveling. My dislikes are not too many; I don't even know that you can really call them dislikes though because I have never really given them much of a chance. Those are ice skating, skiing and fishing. And here is the big one, let's see, what I am I looking for in a man, well, I would have to say, that I am looking for a man who is non-judgmental, can accept me for who I am and not try to change me into someone I am not. I would like a man who is not only caring, loving and considerate but also very respectful. One who is looking for a long term relationship and not just out for a one night stand or a sex partner. That is my story and I am sticking to it, as I start to laugh."

John says, "Wow, well looks like we are both looking for the same things in life."

"Can I ask you why you are even remotely interested in me, when there is so much distance between the two of us? I think, to be honest with you, it will be a big problem. I just don't think I can have a long distance relationship. I would like to be able to be with my man more than just on weekends every once in a while. I don't think they ever work out unless one of us would be willing to move. And I really don't see that happening", I answered.

"Well, my feeling is that time and distance makes the heart and love grows stronger. So I am really sorry that you feel that way, because I really think we can make this work for us regardless of the distance between the two of us", he responded.

After all the anxiety and nerves, I hate to say it, but I just don't know if this date will ever amount to anything more than just that, a date. I guess we will see though. John has to go back to his home tomorrow and I have no idea whether I will ever talk to him or see him again, but at least I went out and met with him, which was a very big step for me to take. I can only hope that I will, but if I don't, that is okay. As I said before, I am by far not ready for any long term relationship yet, so meeting with John once in a while is fine with me. I am not about to jump right in here with both feet.

As it turns out, I guess John was happy with his first visit and meeting with me, enough anyway so that we continued to talk online.

When he got back home he called and said, "Hi Margie, I just wanted to call you and thank you for a great time."

I replied, "I had a great time to John. Thanks for a really nice evening. It has been a very long time since I laughed and had such a nice night."

"Well, I am glad that you did, he answered.

"Well, it is late and I have a very long day tomorrow and have to get up early. So I will talk to you tomorrow. You have a nice evening and have sweet dreams. Good Night." "Good night John and thanks again. Talk to you later. Bye."

"Bye" John said.

So we had continued talking to each other over the next couple of weeks. Everything seemed to be going well.

John had called and asked me, "I want to know if I can meet up with you again this weekend?"

I answered, "Of course John, I would really like to see you again." And so we did and we had a wonderful evening of dancing this time.

It was morning, and John had to catch his flight to go back home. These days have become really hard to say good bye again. Until the relationship is to change somehow, we are learning to deal with it though. It is really hard to let go at the end of the weekends.

In all of our talks and learning more about each other, I had learned that John worked with computers and subcontracting for the government offices in and around Washington D.C. So, he is a very intelligent and computer savvy man, which I certainly was not.

What I didn't know at first was that John had been hacking into my computer. He knew everything about me. He knew what sites that I had been going into and pretty much everything that I do online. He had been going into the history and the recent sites that I had visited. He slipped up a couple of times and that was how I had figured out what he was doing while he was back home. I guess that he thought that because we had seen each other a few times that I was his and I was not supposed to meet or date any other man. In my opinion, he has a lot of nerve. I can't even believe that he would do this.

Here I thought that he was a great guy. Now I find out he is nothing more than a control freak. Well I sure don't need this in my life. So any kind of relationship that we may or may not have had is gone now. I just, absolutely, refuse to go any further in a relationship with John now.

I slept on all of this last night and am hopefully ready to deal with John when he calls today, and I know that he will. I am so down and so depressed about all of this. I don't understand why some people feel the need to control others. I will never understand it. Is it their own insecurities, or is it just that they think or know that they can get away with that kind of behavior. Either way, I won't put up with it.

Well, just as I had expected, he is calling me now.

"Hello," I answered.

"Hi Margie, I have been trying to get a hold of you for the past couple of days and you haven't answered me. Is everything okay? I have seen that you have been online, but you haven't answered any of my messages, how come?"

I responded to John, "Well, to be perfectly honest with you, I haven't wanted to talk to you John. As far as you knowing I have been online, I know that you know when I am online and what I am doing because you have hacked into my computer, and please do not deny it. Because I know it is true."

"Why do you think that?" he asked.

"Please do not play me for a fool. I know you have, because you have slipped a couple of times asking me questions about sites that I have visited. I am not stupid John. I can put two and two together."

"I swear Margie, I haven't. I can't, I don't have the capability to do something like that" he explained.

"Yes you do and you have. With your knowledge of computers and the fact that you work for the government, you can and you have. So we are done. You need to stop it or I will have no other choice but to report you for hacking into my computer which could affect your job and I am sure that you do not want that. So just leave me alone now. No more calls, texts, or online messages. What we had is gone. There is nothing now. I hope that you find what you are looking for, but I will not ever be controlled by any man. Bye John", I said.

"Wait a minute, can we talk about this before you shut me out?"

"No John, there is nothing else to say or talk about. I said what I needed to say to you."

"Well don't I get a chance to explain?", he asked. "No, there is nothing to explain. No explanation you have can justify what you have done. I mean what I say, it is over."

"Well, I already bought the airline tickets to come be with you next weekend. So what am I supposed to do with them? They are nonrefundable."

"Well I am sorry about that, but I don't want to see you anymore and that is that. Bye John."

CHAPTER 6

Alone Again

So here I am again, all alone and depressed with no relationship. I have no one and nothing to look forward to in my life except loneliness and boredom. I would rather be alone though than to be in a very controlling long distance relationship anyways. I deserve better than that. What is wrong with me? Why is it that I fell for, once again, another man who thinks that I am so stupid and naïve that I can be controlled? Am I that pathetic? What do I need to do to get beyond all of these situations in my relationships that have such a devastating hold over me?

Obviously, I still have a lot of work to do on myself to overcome these feelings of worthlessness. I have absolutely no confidence in myself at all if I keep allowing this to happen to me. I just don't know what I can do to get beyond all of this. I am not comfortable with going out anywhere to meet new people yet. With as shy as I am, it is almost impossible for me to initiate conversations with people that I don't know or ones that I have just met. Usually, I will just go and sit there and not talk to anyone at all. That is just the way that I am and have always been. I continue to see my therapist, because I still need so much more help.

In my free time, I started searching the internet; mostly just to have something to do. I also hoped that maybe I would be able to let go of some of the fears in my life. I found some of the singles sites.

Just out of curiosity, I signed up for one of them, especially since it was free and wouldn't cost me anything. So in order to sign up though, I had to build a profile about myself. Putting in the profile a nickname, city where I live, my likes, and dislikes and also what I am looking for on the site, whether it would be just for friends, a casual relationship or a long term one, and other things.

It was to let everyone know a little about me, and what I am all about. It was pretty interesting, but it was also hard trying to figure out what to write about myself to make it interesting enough for others to possibly want to meet with me. Not an easy thing to do considering how I am feeling about myself right now.

So now I am done with that. Wow, was that ever a challenge for me to do. Now what? I said to myself. Do I just wait and see what happens or am I going to be brave enough to start browsing for other singles in my area?

Margie Garrett

I am so unsure of myself; however, I also know that I need to get past all of the insecure feelings that I have. Scared? You bet that I am. I am not really sure that I will ever gain my self-respect or confidence back in my life. I know one thing though, and that is that I really need to try very hard otherwise, I am not going anywhere, and might as well just give up. However, if I do that, than I will be all alone for the rest of my life and that, for sure, is not what I want to happen? I really don't.

I just have to keep telling myself the same thing over and over again about how it will be if I can only change the way I am and have been for way too long in my life. If I don't make an effort, than I am destined to be miserable and depressed for the rest of my life.

My walls are just so high; it is going to take a while for any man to break them down. I don't know that I will ever break them down all of the way to let another man in. I really don't want to be hurt again like I have so many times in my past. I admit that a lot of the hurt is my own fault though. I did allow another man to get close to me. I let those walls down and I wasn't ready to do that. I did it though. I just need to learn from my mistakes and not make the same mistakes again. It is really going to be a long time for me to let another man get close to me that way.

Stepping out of my comfort zone is one thing, but I won't be letting my walls down for quite some time. I just can't do it. I am too afraid of being hurt again. It will really be hard for a man to even remotely get close to me now. I almost feel sorry for the poor sucker, because I have become really hardened after everything that I have been through.

CHAPTER 7

Stepping Out Of My Comfort Zone

I had decided last night, that I was going to challenge myself and see what happens. So, I went on the singles site and started browsing the other single men in the area. I pretty much just wanted to see who was out there and what they were looking for. I couldn't believe some of the profiles that I had read. Some of these men were really something else. Honest, I will say that. They were very explicit in what they were looking for and what they want out of a woman. And then some of the others you could tell were either very shy or reserved, or they themselves had been abused in one way or another by their past relationships. It was actually a very interesting night to say the least. And, yes, men can have the abusive relationships just like woman. I have seen and heard a lot of horror stories from both men and woman. I just couldn't believe some of the profiles that I had read. Wow. This is just so unbelievable.

Margie Garrett

I also, could not even believe the responses that I had received from my own profile. The response, to say the least, was really overwhelming. This was my first day on the site and I already had over one hundred messages from men that were interested in meeting or talking with me. I didn't want to be rude by not responding back to them. It took me almost an entire day just reading all of the messages and responding back. I had no idea, what to say, so I mostly just kept it short and thanked them for their interest in me. Then, I just waited to see if any of them ever responded back and showed further interest. I guess time will tell. I was actually pretty scared that they would. This is a very big step out of my comfort zone for sure. The mere thought of meeting a new man or others in general is going to be so hard. I just don't know if I am ready for this at all.

I decided over the next few days, that I would just continue to visit the site and browse. I started to read some of the forums and the other areas of the site. It was really very interesting what some people would share about themselves or their thoughts and feelings about certain subjects. After visiting the site over the last several days, I also noticed that there are singles parties going on around the area. Pretty interesting because I can go into the party thread and see exactly who has signed up for the party and who will be there. They go into the party thread and make certain comments about how they are glad to see a certain someone is coming and just chat in there.

The next party was only a couple of weeks away. I have no friends to go with, being that all of my friends had left me through the divorce process. I literally had to start my life all over again with no friends at all. I wasn't sure what to do. I really do want to go, but not by myself. That is for sure. I just don't know that I can go there alone. I have never walked into a bar by myself in my whole life. And now, I know that for me to meet anyone, male or female, I am going to have to go somewhere to meet new people. I had decided that I was going to try and bring myself enough courage to at least try to go and see what they are like. I have two weeks to prepare myself for it. I don't know about this. Can I get enough courage and strength together to do this?

Over the next couple of weeks in preparation, I went out shopping to buy something nice to wear for the party. I made an appointment to get my hair done, all so that I would look good. Also, in preparation, so that I didn't feel totally alone and not have anyone to talk to, I did start talking to some of the singles that were going so that I wouldn't feel too uncomfortable, and so that I would have some singles to sit and talk with.

Margie Garrett

How these last couple of weeks have flown by. Here I go. It is the morning of the big night. I am so nervous and anxious about all of this. In some respects, I feel crippled by my own anxieties and insecurities about whether or not I can actually make this happen in going to this party and meeting a lot of new people. I just keep telling myself throughout the day, that I can do this. Trying so hard to convince myself of it was another story though.

As the day went on, I became more anxious every minute. It is about time for me to get ready, and all I could think of was that I must be totally crazy for even considering doing this. However, I also didn't want to let my nerves stop me from doing what I needed to do. I sure didn't want my nerves and anxiety to hold me back. I am strong and I can do this. That is what I kept telling myself over and over again.

Here I go. I am all dressed up for the party, makeup is on, hair is done and I look one last time in the mirror. I said to myself, okay this is it. I get into my jeep heading out to the party for what I thought was going to be a party of about two hundred singles. When I arrived there, I looked at the parking lot and said to myself, "Oh My God, what am I doing?" The parking lot was completely full and they were actually walking from parked cars down the street. There were so many singles that people were standing outside, because you couldn't even walk inside. I drove by and came back for a second attempt to go. I drove by again. I did that about four times and then finally just gave up and went home. I was so disgusted with myself for not going in. I guess I was just too intimidated and not ready for this yet. I still, obviously, have some work on my self-confidence to do.

It seems it is going to be a while for me to feel comfortable with any of this. I will in time though, I really will. I have to make this happen. After all, I don't want to be alone for the rest of my life, now do I?

I now have at least another couple of weeks before the next party. I really have to bring myself to go to the next one, or else the frustration level is going to be way too high. I have two weeks to talk to other females that I might be able to go with. At least until I can build up enough self-confidence to go by myself and not be afraid.

I just continue to browse, chat and try and make some online friends for now. I never heard from John again and that was a good thing, because I no longer had to deal with all of his lies and deceit not to mention his online stalking.

I did start getting some replies from the men who had originally messaged me. They asked me if I had gone to the party, because they didn't see me there. The one guy I wanted to meet ended up not going anyways. I messaged him the day after the party, and yeah, I know I am starting to get a little bit braver as the days go on.

I asked, "Carlos, I see that you didn't go to the party last night either. I couldn't get through the door last night even if I wanted too. It was so packed, and I guess I just wasn't really comfortable with going into a place where I really knew no one anyways."

He replied back to me and said, "Yeah, I here you there. I couldn't go last night because I was called in to work. Duty calls. I would still like to meet you soon though. Maybe when my schedule lightens up a little, we could get together for a cup of coffee?"

"I would like that, just let me know when."

"I will do that." He replied.

So it seems that I won't be meeting Carlos for a while anyway, so it is time to move on to one of the others that showed interest.

Well, it is getting late tonight, so I think I am going to shut down the computer and try to get some sleep. At least I am going to try to. My brain is just racing with all of these thoughts and emotions, on top of the fact that I have been in a lot of pain all day from the Crohn's Disease. Hopefully, tomorrow will be a better day for me. I can only hope.

I tried, but it seems that all I am doing is tossing and turning, so I took a pain pill, which I really don't like to do. Sometimes though, I just do not have any choice in the matter. For the most part, I just try to deal with the pain and not let it affect my daily living, but sometimes it is just impossible to do it. I do try so hard. I have learned to hide my pain very well, so that family and friends usually never see how much pain I am actually in. I do a good job, I must admit, but I just don't want it to take control of my life. And so far I have been able to do that. I don't really have any choice, now do I, especially, if I want to be happy. After taking the pill, I was able to finally fall off asleep. I didn't sleep real well, but at least I did sleep.

Margie Garrett

It's now another day. What am I going to do? First things are first. I have to have my morning coffee. And then I usually boost my laptop up and check all of my messages. It looks like it is going to be a beautiful, warm and sunny day today. In checking all of my messages, there was one from a guy named Gary. His message said that he would like to meet me and left his phone number for me to call him. Oh, yeah, right! What do I do now? Do I call him? Or do I just ignore the message all together. I can't be that rude, especially, when I got on this site to eventually meet other single men and woman.

I finished my coffee and worked up the nerve to call Gary. So here I go, I can't even believe that I am actually doing this.

"Hi Gary, this is Margie, I got your message wanting me to call you. How are you this morning?"

Gary said, "I am great, what an absolutely gorgeous day this is. I think that I am going to go work on my boat for a while and maybe this afternoon I will take it out. So what are you up to today?"

I said, "I actually have no plans at all today except maybe some work around here."

"Well, I would really like to meet you today if you aren't busy. How do you feel about boats and the water?"

"I love them."

"Well how do you feel about coming out to my boat on the water and maybe meeting me today for a while?"

I had replied, "I would really like that, I haven't been out on a boat in a very long time. Sounds like a lot of fun."

"Well then how soon can you get out here? We can make a day of it."

I wasn't really sure about how I felt about spending the entire day with a guy I have never met, so I had said to him,

"Well, how about I come meet you for a cup of coffee first and go from there. You might not want to be stuck with me all day you know."

He replied, "Okay, fair enough."

I got the directions from him and he met me up at the dock at a little restaurant. He seems like a really nice guy. We had a cup of coffee and talked for a while, mostly about the singles sites and his experiences with the woman he had met on there. After talking, he asked me, "So, what do you think, do you want to go see my boat?" I said, "Sure, I would like to see it." And so we walked over to his boat. Wow it was really nice too. So, we went onboard and he took me out on the water. What a beautiful day for a boat ride.

Things seem to be going well and as I said, he seemed like a really nice guy.

I was having a great time until he threw the anchor out, and said to me, "Let's go down in the cabin and have a beer."

I said, "Sure, okay."

Margie Garrett

That was a big mistake. I shouldn't have gone down below. For one, it was in the very early afternoon. I should have taken that as a warning sign, but I didn't. All of the sudden, I started to get very anxious. Not knowing what his intentions were. Or what he expected from me. He took his shirt off, but it was sunny and warm, so I really didn't think much of it.

Then a few minutes later, he said to me, "I hope you don't mind, but I am a nudist and don't wear clothes any more than I have to. And being, that we are way a ways from shore, I usually go nude. You can join me if you would like to."

I couldn't believe my eyes. I was in total shock. He was now, nothing like I had expected, hoped or thought that he was. Now what do I do or say to this one? Wow, I can't believe that I put myself in this position. How utterly stupid I feel right now. All I know is, I am surely not going to take my clothes off for him. I fear rape now, and am really scared and full of anxiety. I have to say something to him, but what, is the question.

So I said, "Gary, I am really sorry, but no I am not going to take my clothes off and I think that maybe you should just take me back to the dock. I didn't know that you were a nudist. I am just not feeling comfortable at all now."

"Okay, sorry, but this is who I am", he said to me.

"I really am sorry Gary, but I am sure that you will find a lady that can be that way. It just isn't me at all."

So Gary took me back to the dock, and we said our goodbyes. I left for home very quickly, I might add. I really couldn't get away from him fast enough. It wasn't that he wasn't handsome, nice or respectful in every other way, because he was. He is who he is, just like I am who I am, and that is not a nudist. I am just so thankful that he was respectful and understanding enough to not do anything to hurt me. He certainly had the opportunity to if he wanted to force himself on me, being that we were miles from shore and no one in sight to help me out of what, in reality, was a very dangerous situation. I was a very lucky lady.

After that date, I was so depressed and full of anxiety. I had been shaking and not sure about this dating scene at all now. Dating is so much more dangerous than it was years ago. You just don't know what to expect as far as your safety goes. It makes me really wonder, whether I really want to date again after this one. I am so leery now of meeting any guy. I know that there has to be some good guys out there somewhere. Talk about some slim pickings though. The good men seem to be very far and few between.

In checking my messages again, I have an awful lot of them, but some of them are from out of state and even from out of the country. I have had a couple from Mexico and some from France and Canada also.

Margie Garrett

I don't know why these men are looking for woman out of their own states let alone going outside of their countries. What kind of a relationship would that be? I had already tried dating a guy from out of state, and it was not only hard, but didn't work for me at all. I guess, I just want a relationship with a man that is local. Picky aren't I? I want to be able to talk and see him more often than if he lived far away.

Oh, I would talk to them and even meet with them, but it will be for friendship only. I had so many messages again. This will keep me busy for this evening anyway. I hope I have a message from at least one of the ladies I sent a message too about going to this next party.

As I go through these messages, I still keep saying to myself, What in the world am I doing? Why am I putting myself through all of this? Is this really going to be worth it? Will I really ever be able to find a good man this way? I just don't know. Some of these men's profiles are something else. Talk about being completely blunt with what they are looking for in a woman. I am lucky if I find a couple of men in the hundreds of messages that I would even remotely be interested in meeting. The more that I look; the more depressed and discouraged I become. Pretty much all of the men, I get the impression; just want a one night stand of fun and sex, and nothing more than that. They certainly are not looking for a long term relationship.

Great, I have a message from one of the woman, Donna is her name. She left me her phone number to call her about going to the upcoming party, which is to take place next Saturday. She said to call her tonight after six o'clock.

So I called her. "Hi Donna, this is Margie, how are you today?"

"Hi Margie, I am doing okay. Have you been able to go to any of the singles parties yet? I haven't convinced myself to go yet. I really don't want to go to one of them alone not knowing anyone there, or what they would be like. I am hoping that they aren't like walking into a meat market where all of the guys act like they have only one thing in mind for the night. I just hope that there are some men that will be going for the same reason that we are. So did you find someone to go with you yet? Or do you have a date for the night yet?"

I responded, "No, I met a guy this afternoon and had hoped that maybe I would have a date, but the date turned out to be a total disaster."

"You are kidding me, what happened?" she asked.

"He seemed like such a nice guy, and he had asked me this afternoon if I wanted to go for a boat ride, and of course, I said yes. We met at the dock restaurant first and I felt okay about him. So I went with him. We were miles away from the shore, when he informed me that he is a nudist. He started taking his clothes off."

"Oh My God, what did you do?" she asked.

"I told him I wasn't going to be removing mine and to just please take me back to the dock. And that was the end of that meeting."

"You are so lucky you know."

"Yeah, I know. Anything could have happened this afternoon. I was so scared; I didn't know what to do for fear of what he might do to me. I took my chance that is for sure. So did you find someone to go to the party with you yet?"

"No, I haven't. Are you still going to go?"

"Yes, I would like to. I am not going by myself. If I do, I think I want to go early for dinner and so that I can get good seating. Would you like to meet me maybe in an hour or so early for dinner?" she asked.

"That sounds like a really good idea, because I tried going to the last one and just couldn't bring myself to even park the Jeep, let alone go in. Guess I am just not that brave yet and with not knowing any others there to feel comfortable about even going in by myself. Maybe, later I might be able to, but not anytime soon I am sure. So what time do you think that we should meet up there if the party starts at nine o'clock?"

"I think probably around seven o'clock or so should be good. What do you think?"

"That sounds good to me."

"Okay, good. Well I need to get off of here and get some sleep. I have another long day tomorrow. It was nice talking to you Margie. I will talk to you later."

"Okay, have a good night Donna."

I went back to checking my messages and finished up with them a couple of hours later. I had such a stressful and potentially dangerous day today. I know one thing, I won't be going on anymore boat rides until I have met and had at least a couple of dates with the guy first. I just won't to put myself through that danger again. Live and Learn. I need to be more careful. I need to try harder to not put myself into any more of those stressful situations. It only causes me to be sicker and have more problems with my Crohn's, and I certainly don't need that.

Well it's the start of a new day. What will happen today? Hopefully, it will just be a relaxing day for me. I need a stress free day after all the craziness that happened to me yesterday. So, as I wake up this morning, I am going to be conscious and put all of those anxious thoughts and fear to the side. All the anxious thoughts do is keep the worry and fear alive in me, and I don't want that in my life.

And so as I start my morning, I am going to do some browsing through some of the profiles just out of curiosity. I certainly was in no means, ready to approach and write to any of them though. As I was browsing through them, I received an instant message from a man online. We started talking as I looked at his profile. I saw his picture and noticed his age. I didn't believe that his picture was recent. He just looked awfully young in it, compared to what he said that his age was. His name is Carl.

So I asked Carl, "So is that a recent picture of you?"

Carl replied, "Well it was taken about a year or so ago. Why do you ask?"

"Because, you look so young in it, almost like it is an old picture. Do you have a more recent one of you that you can send to my email while we talk? I just like to see who I am talking too."

"Sure, that is not a problem. I will send it to you right now."

And so he did. I opened up my mail and looked at the picture and I couldn't believe my eyes. The picture looked nothing like the other man in the original picture at all.

So I asked, "Okay Carl, I looked at it and here is a million dollar question for you. Which of these pictures are really you? The one here or the one you just sent me, because these pictures show two totally different men."

Next thing I know, Carl had closed out the chat window. Neither one of the pictures, obviously, were him. Apparently, I caught him in a lie. And he knew that, and just didn't know how to react or what to say to me. So he said nothing. I never heard from him again.

I will never understand why people are so dishonest with the pictures that they put on the site as portraying themselves, whether it is another person or a picture that was taken years ago. Do they think that we won't eventually see that? Better yet, what do they think our reaction will be when we meet them for the first time, especially, when I expect that they will look like their picture?

I have met some men that claimed that they were fit only to find out that they were way overweight too. It just won't get them anywhere with me to lie. And if they are going to lie about their own looks, what else are they going to be lying about. Really makes me wonder if I could ever trust that anything that they say is the truth or just another lie.

I continued browsing through the profiles and reading all of the comments made by various different singles, both men and woman, about the upcoming party this weekend in the chat forums on the singles site. Still totally amazed as to what these men put on their profiles. Some of the men will say that they are married and looking, some say that they are separated, while others say, it is complicated, some say single. It's unbelievable as far as the married men, especially when this is a singles site. We all know, that the only reason that they are here, is because they can take advantage of a vulnerable woman. Some men will even say the reason that they are on the site is for a sexual encounter. Guess that is being about as honest as you can get. Unbelievable.

CHAPTER 8

Dating and Anxiety

In remembering my date with Gary and the boat ride, I became even more anxious and depressed. Not knowing if I will ever be able to find a man or if I will be alone forever. I know that I shouldn't be thinking about any of this. My heart is racing to the point where I can actually count the heartbeats, and my thoughts just seem to be going crazy with the fear of being alone. The mere thought of anymore dates scares me too. I feel like I am so fearful all of the time. Right now, I feel like I am having a panic attack. This is something that I have to learn to overcome, but the question is how I do it though. If I don't continue to try to go to meet new people, than I will never get over the fear and anxious thoughts of being alone, so I need to keep trying to.

So I continue on the dating site. Why, you ask? Well, sometimes, I don't really know, and then other times, because of wanting to get over some of my anxiety and fears of being alone, with no friends, male or female.

I received another message from yet another man. His name is Tim. We emailed back and forth over the next couple of days. It was the day before the party now.

Tim asked me, "So Margie, are you going to the party tomorrow night?"

I replied, "Yes, I am meeting up there early with a lady friend. I figure we would go early, get a good seat and have some dinner before the party starts. Why do you ask?" "Well, because I am thinking about going, and I would really like to meet you there." I said to Tim, "That would be great."

Well, it is morning, and the day of the party. All of the fear and anxious thoughts are now racing. Will I look good? Will I be able to actually do this? What will people be saying about me? I am not a pretty lady, and I am sure there are going to be so many that are. I feel like I just don't even have a chance of meeting a man. Probably won't be approached by any of them anyways, so I am feeling even more depressed. I feel like, no matter how good my hair and makeup look, it won't really matter. I know, I should be going with a positive attitude, but I am just not positive about myself right now, let alone meeting others. Full of fear and anxious thoughts this morning, that is for sure. I have to do this though, if I ever have a chance of overcoming these thoughts and fears. I have too.

I went to the beautician and had her do my hair for the party. Then I had to find something nice to wear to this party, which was a task in itself, beings that I really don't have anything other than jeans to wear. I did manage to at least find a nice top to wear with them though.

I called Donna, "Hey Donna, are you all ready for the party tonight? We are still meeting up there for dinner, Right"

And Donna replied, "Yes, I am a little nervous about going, but I guess if we get up there early enough, I will be okay. So are we still meeting up there around seven o'clock tonight?"

"Yes, I think that is good. That will give us enough time to have something to eat before we start drinking. I don't know about you, but I need some food in my stomach, if I know that I am going to be drinking. I know how you feel about being nervous, so am I. I have been talking with this guy the last couple of days and said that he wants to meet me up there. I am a nervous wreck, especially after the last date that I had."

"Well, hopefully, he will be a good guy."

"I sure hope so."

And so we met up there and had a good dinner. It was about a half an hour before the party begins. The singles were all starting to come in. By the time of the party, there were no seats left in the place.

Some of the singles were actually standing around because of the crowd. The place was completely packed. You can barely dance on the dance floor. It wasn't going anywhere with me though, as far as meeting any of the single men. Not that there weren't any here, but none of them approached me. I felt completely lost and depressed. Like a real looser.

I said to Donna "Tim said that he was coming tonight. Where is he? It is almost midnight already and he hasn't come yet. Guess, he really didn't want to meet me or he had something better to do tonight. Oh well, story of my life."

"Well, maybe he had to work late tonight or something came up that he couldn't make it."

"Yeah, I suppose. I am just really disappointed. It is almost one o'clock already, and I have had not one guy even talk to me, so I think that I am just going to call it a night and go home. I am so depressed. I was really hoping that this party would be better. Do I look that bad?"

"No, you look great. I have no idea why most of the men are standing over there like wallflowers."

"Well, I am sure not going to go over there to them. Call me old fashion, but that is just the way that I am. I can't do that."

"I know, I can do that either."

"It will be interesting to see if Tim ever contacts me again."

So we had both left the party. Both of us very discouraged. I didn't know if I even wanted to go to the next one, because of what tonight was like. Really, why bother, because with the exception of the band being really good, I didn't even get a chance to dance.

I just went home and crawled into my bed all depressed and really not even caring if I wake up the next morning to face another day of the same thing, all of the depression, anxiety, anger and fear of life in general. I do know that in order to overcome these fears, I have to continue to try to have some form of a social life. Just don't know if I ever will, but I do need to keep trying.

The next morning I woke up though, still very depressed and disappointed in everything. I fixed myself my coffee and sat and watched the news, rather than going online. I just couldn't do it this morning. I figured, maybe, I would just take a break from all of it for at least a little while. So instead, I watched the news and played some online games. I really didn't care if I had gone on the site today at all.

It was afternoon, before I finally decided to go online and check to see if I had any messages, and much to my surprise, there was a message from Tim asking me to call him. I have absolutely no clue why I should, beings that I felt like I was sort of stood up. After all, he did ask me if I would be there to meet him at the part, and then he didn't even show up, not even for a few minutes to meet me.

I did call him though. "Hi Tim, you asked me to call you. What's up?"

I know, I sounded kind of rude, but I was still so upset.

He said, "Margie, I wanted you to call so that I could apologize to you for not making it to the party. I had to work late last night. I really am sorry."

I now felt really horrible. Just thinking that he had changed his mind and had met someone else and decided to just go somewhere else last night.

I said to him, "It is okay Tim, don't worry about it. The party was okay, except it seemed most all of the men acted like wall flowers last night, so I ended up leaving early."

"That is a shame, because most of them are pretty good. It must have been an off night for everyone then."

"I suppose so."

"So do you still want to meet me? We could go get a cup of coffee or something. I really do want to meet you."

I said, "Sure, we can do that. There is a restaurant down the street from me. We could meet up there. What time would you like to meet?"

"Well, I have to get changed first, so how about three o'clock?"

"Three o'clock sounds good, I will see you then."

"Okay, see you in a little bit. Bye"

I don't look nearly as good as I did last night. So he sees me as I am today. I put some makeup and cologne on and just wore jeans and a nice top to go meet with him. That is the best that I can do. I don't have much of a wardrobe. You might say that I don't really have one at all. Pretty much, just a couple of jeans and shirts, which is really all I can afford. I am sure not dressed up today. So, like I said, he sees the real me today. I am who I am. What can I say? I sure don't get enough money to go out and buy new clothes for dates. Some of these women go get their hair done, get manicures, pedicures and spend an awful lot of money to impress the guy. I just can't see doing that. If a guy doesn't like me for who I am, the personally he isn't worth pursuing a relationship with. I just don't see the point in it.

So I had finished getting ready and went to the restaurant to meet Tim. He met me at the car.

I said, "Hi Tim."

"Hey Margie, so how has your morning been?"

"It has been good."

"So are you ready to go in for some coffee?"

"Yes I am."

And so we went into the restaurant, and the waitress seated us and asked,

"What can I get the both of you to drink?"

Tim said to the waitress, "I think we are both going to have some coffee."

She said, "Okay, I will be right back with your coffee."

So we started talking to each other, mostly about how the party was.

Tim asked me, "So did you have a good time at the party last night? Was this your first one or have you gone to any others"

I said, "It was okay, the band was really good. I guess I just expected it to be better than it was. I didn't get to even dance one song. So it was pretty disappointing to me. Everyone made them out to be so much fun. I guess the parties are what you make them out to be. Things are just so much different now than they were years ago though, where the guys were the ones that approached the woman, and not the other way around. I don't know if I could ever be that way. Society has changed so much from when I was young. And I really never know what to expect when I meet you guys. Some men are very honest and respectful, and others are very dishonest, deceitful and have absolutely no respect. It really is kind of dangerous for us. I have already had one bad experience. I can only live and learn what to do in these situations."

"I know, I feel the same way about the woman. I had a lady that I wanted to meet. I talked with her a few times. She was very pretty in her picture and very nice. So I decided to meet with her, like you, just for some coffee at first. It turned out that her picture was very old and she was at least one hundred pounds overweight."

"Oh my, what did you do?"

Margie Garrett

"The respectful think, I stayed and had coffee with her. When I got home though, I sent her a message saying that she is a very nice lady, but that she needs to get an updated picture on her profile. Then I never contacted her again. Call me horrible, but there has to be some physical attraction too. Don't you think?"

"Yes, and she sure should not have portrayed in her picture a slim average lady. She is being very dishonest."

"Oh and here is another one for you. I had met this woman and as we were leaving, she said she wanted me to meet one of her lady friends. It turned out that she had been waiting in the parking lot for us to come out. So we went up to her and she asked us where the closes motel was so that we could have our own little intimate party of some fun and sex. I asked them if they were kidding me. They said that they weren't, and I said to them that not only will I not have sex with them but that I would never engage in any threesome with them, and that I hope they find a guy, but it sure wasn't going to be me and to have a good night. Then I just walked away from the both of them. Can you believe that one?"

"I am so sorry Tim, but please don't judge all of us ladies. Not all of us are that way. Really we aren't. Unbelievable what they had expected from you that night."

We went on and on about some of our experiences. We had totally lost track of time. He is really a nice guy from what I can tell.

He walked me to my car and said, "So, can I see you again?"

"I would like that." "Maybe the next time, I will take you out dancing. You do like to dance right?"

"Yes I do."

"Okay, well I will get a hold of you, and we can make plans to do that then."

"Great, I will talk to you soon then."

I really, to be honest, didn't think that he would ever ask me out again. I have no self-confidence. I lost all of that long ago. I still have an awful lot of work to do on myself. Don't I?

Later that afternoon, Donna had called and asked me, "So what did you think of your first party? Did Tim ever contact you today?"

"Yes, he did this morning. He asked me to call him when I got the message. So I called him, turns out that he wanted to apologize for not going to the party. He said he was called into work. We ended up meeting for coffee earlier."

"Really? And how did that go?"

"It went pretty good. He asked me if I wanted to go dancing one day soon."

"What did you say to him?"

"I told him that I would like that."

Margie Garrett

"Do you think he will call you again?"

"Who knows, but I am certainly not waiting around for a relationship that might end up being mostly friendship. I am just not going to do it."

"I don't blame you there."

"So are you going to the next party? Hopefully, this next one will be better."

"When is the next one?"

"It will be in a couple of weeks. There is a party at least twice a month if they can."

"I more than likely will go. What about you? Are you going to go? Maybe we should do the same thing, go early and get a good seat again."

"Yes, that works for me."

"Can I ask you something Donna?"

"Sure, what is it?"

"Is it me, am I the only one that seems to attract all the morons. I have met some weird men out there."

"No, you aren't alone, I have had some guys that would meet me, and one of the first things that come out of their mouth is asking me where there is a hotel. Can you believe the bluntness in these men that only want a one night stand? I am sure there is some woman out there that would like that, but I am looking for a long term relationship and not a sexual encounter. Do these men just look at the pictures and not even bother to read our profiles to find out what we are looking for in a man. I guess that most men have a one tract mind, and don't think about anything else but getting laid. It just totally drives me nuts. I never know which one is a good one or which one just wants to have sex. How can I tell? I have absolutely no idea. I am as in the dark about all of this as you are."

Margie Garrett

You pretty much take your chances with meeting these guys and learn to be very careful to protect yourself. Sometimes it is so hard though, because some men are just so unpredictable. You just never know. Looking online for men is something that I never thought I would do, but let's face it, where else are you supposed to go if you don't go to the bars. I just refuse to do that by myself. That would be way too uncomfortable for me to do. You can't exactly meet a guy in the store and strike up an interesting conversation.

So this is why I am trying the online singles sites. I just get really tired of talking to, and going out meeting these guys, only to be set up for disappointments over and over again. However, I continue trying. I know that there has to be some good guys out there. Where are you? I think you are all in hiding. They, to, are probably tired of trying to find a good woman. I hope that Time will call me again, but I am certainly to going to wait around to see. Even if he does, I don't have any idea whether it would ever go past the first date.

So, I continue looking and meeting other men. As I check my messages again, I did get one from Tim. He wants to take me out on Saturday. I did meet with Dave. He was okay. I might go out with him again to see if I feel any more of a connection to him.

He asked me, "Margie, I am barbecuing some steaks tonight, would you like to come over for dinner and we can watch a movie?"

I said, "Okay, what time?"

"I think around six o'clock would be good."

So I went over and everything was fine. I was there for about a couple of hours and then I went home. I still didn't know what to think about him.

I am just getting so tired lately. I know that it is all of the depression and anxiety that has been hitting me so hard. I am having a really hard time dealing with all of this. All of the financial worries, my health, and of just going home alone every night with no one to talk to and really nothing to do to keep my mind off of all of it. I just feel like I could literally sleep my life away, if I could only sleep. I can't though, because of my mind constantly racing and all of the pain that I experience every day now. Why has my life been so hard? Why do I have to go from day to day with what seems to be no light at the end of the tunnel? I still feel like I can never seem to get ahead enough to be happy. I do have my good days, but it just seems like my bad days definitely far way the good ones. I am just so tired of being depressed all of the time.

After going home and checking my messages, I had received one from Tim. He asked if he could come to my place on Thursday. I don't normally do this, but we had seen each other at least a couple of times and I did feel comfortable with him, so I had told him that he could come over. We had continued to see each other over the next couple of weeks.

Margie Garrett

I became sick again with my Crohn's Disease and it was mostly because of all of the financial stress that I had been under. I had no food to speak of in the house. Tim had come over to comfort me and saw that I had no food in the freezer or refrigerator. He usually doesn't come over two days in a row. The next day though he did come over again. He knocked on my door. When I had answered, he had a couple of bags of groceries. He set them down in my kitchen, and went back to his truck to get the rest. I couldn't believe my eyes. I just couldn't believe that he had done that for me. He didn't even know me that well. He did though. I was so grateful simply because I was so hungry. I hadn't had much to eat over the last few days. Mostly I just had some broth and noodles which was about all I could afford. He sat with me for a little while then gave me a kiss goodbye, said that he had to get up early for work.

Later that evening, Dave had called me and asked me if I would like to go over there for a beer this weekend. I said that I would like that and that it sounds like a plan. He said that we could just chill out and watch a movie. I said sounded good, like a nice relaxing evening. He had said that he can make me really relaxed holding me. How naïve I am. I didn't think anything of that comment. I just wanted so much to not be alone anymore.

So I went over there. We sat on the sofa; he put his arm around me as we watched the movie. Dave started getting touchy feely as he kissed me. I started to feel a little uncomfortable and I had pulled away a little bit. He moved closer as he asked me if I was okay. And that I just need to relax, that he isn't going to hurt me. I tried to relax, but instead of him helping me to relax, he was making me really uncomfortable and now almost afraid of him and the situation.

I had now become very anxious. He had put his one hand down my shirt to my breast and the other one between my legs. I said to him that I think that I better just go home because it looks like he wants more from me than I will give him. So I had gotten up and went for my purse and walked out of the house.

Margie Garrett

Dave came out and up to me, took the purse out of my hand, slapped me across the face and knocked me down to the ground. As he had me on the ground and was over me, he pulled up my top and started to kiss me and fondle me. He said that I owed him that much, because we had been talking now for weeks. He asked me what I thought that he wanted. I had told him to get off of me and that I didn't owe him anything. He wouldn't stop though. My legs were not pinned and free to move, so I kneed him to get him off of me. It got him away long enough for me to get up and get away.

As I drove home crying, I thought to myself how stupid I was. What in the world is the matter with me? I can't believe that he would just expect that from me. I never gave him any reason to think that I wanted that from him. So needless to say, I was never going to talk to or see Dave again. What is it that I keep attracting the wrong men? I don't understand what I am doing wrong here.

Gary is one persistent guy who is just not giving up. It really makes me wonder why, when I continually put him off on meeting him. He called again and asked me why I won't meet with him. He continues to try and reassure me that he is a nice guy and a gentleman, and that he just doesn't understand what my problem is. I told him that when I feel more comfortable and the time is right then I will meet him. He says he will wait.

I asked him if he was going to the next party, but he said that he doesn't go to the parties. He said he prefers the one on one basis and not with a big crowd. I told him that if he changes his mind that he can meet me there. He said to me that the parties are not for him and that he has absolutely no interest in going to any of them. I said to him that it is too bad. I closed out the conversation just telling him that I had another long day tomorrow and that I will talk to him later and said Goodbye.

There is another singles party next week. I wonder if this one will be any better than the last one.

Tim called me and asked, "Hey, Margie, are you still going to the party next Saturday?"

"Yes I am why do you ask?"

"Well, because it is looking like I might be able to go after all. My boss scheduled me off again."

"That is great. I can't wait to see you again. It has been awhile."

"Yes it has, I have been working a lot of hours lately."

"Well, if you do go will you save a dance for me?"

"Of course I will."

"Good, I am going to hold you to that."

Margie Garrett

I am still not feeling totally comfortable about going to these parties by myself.

I had called and asked Donna, "Are you going to go to the party next week?

"Yes, I am planning on going."

I asked her if she wanted to meet up there early for dinner again and she said she did. We had decided that we would meet up there about the same time which was around seven o'clock again. Donna said to me, "That sounds good."

"Have you had any dates lately? I am about ready to give up. All I seem to get are the morons that only seem to want a one night stand. I had another one that hit me and knocked me down on the ground. I am getting really sick of men and their expectations."

"I am so sorry, you certainly don't deserve this."

"Why can't I just have some happiness in my life for once?"

"You will, you just have to go through all of the rotten men to get to the good ones."

"Well, I am really beginning to wonder whether I will ever find Mr. Right. Maybe, I wasn't born to be happy."

"That is the furthest from the truth. You deserve all the happiness in the world and that is a fact."

"All I know is I am getting to the point of not bothering to look anymore. Let's face it, what good has all of this looking done for me."

"I know Margie, but if you want to be happy then you need to accept and be happy with being alone and fulfill your life in other ways or you need to keep looking for the one man that can bring happiness and love into your life. Otherwise, nothing in your life will ever change."

"Well, I think I might just take a break from all of this, because the first meets and dates are just not worth the danger, depression, anxiety and aggravation anymore."

"Maybe that is a good idea taking a break for a little while. I hate to see you so depressed and unhappy."

I haven't given up on men totally yet. I know that there has to be a good guy somewhere out there for me. I am just tired is all, but I am going to continue looking for now. The party is coming up in a couple of days. I am going to go, but for fun and to meet new singles in the area. However, I am not going to this party to meet any particular man or men. I am going with absolutely no expectations in the world, just to have a good time. I need to get out of this house anyway. Going to this party will help with my confidence issues. Maybe, that is one of my problems with finding the right man.

So, it is the day before the party. What do I wear? You know what, in the past parties, I have been really picky about what I would wear to them. I always try to look my best. So, this time, I think that with the way that I am feeling and my attitude that I have about men in general, I am just going the way I usually always dress and not dress up. If people have a problem with the way that I look, oh well, I am not going to change who I am for any of these men. They either like me for who I am, or I am not going to bother with them anyways.

Oh My God, Gary is calling me again what in the world does he want this time?

"Hello Gary."

"Hi Margie, how are you tonight"

"I am good. I had kind of a rough day today."

"Why is that?"

"I just some problems that came up at work."

"Sorry to hear that."

"Oh, it is okay, nothing unusual. They treat me like this a lot. It just gets really old after a while. So what are you doing this weekend?"

"Remember, I told you I am going to the party. Did you change your mind about going and meeting me there?"

"No, I told you before I don't go to them. What are you doing Sunday then? Any plans?"

"No plans. I am just going to get caught up on some housework"

"Is there any chance of meeting with you?"

"Not a good time for me. I actually am taking a break for a while."

Margie Garrett

"And yet you are going to the party"

"Yes, for fun. I have another call; I have to take this, so I will talk to you later. Bye."

This guy just doesn't know when to take a hint and just give up. I have absolutely no interest in meeting with him at all. You would think he would get the hint. He just doesn't get it though. He is a very persistent guy who obviously doesn't give up until he gets what he wants. So what am I supposed to do here? It is quite obvious that he is not going to go away.

So I finally agreed to meet with him against my better judgment. Gary was one of those men that I had wished I had never given my phone number too. I did though, so now I just have to deal with it. I had hoped he would give up eventually, but he just isn't doing that. So, as much as I didn't want to, but didn't want to be rude to him either, I said that I would meet with him in the afternoon for a quick cup of coffee, because I had a lot of things to do that day. He said that he had hoped that I would come and meet with him closer to his place and get a beer and go to his place a watch a movie. I had agreed to meet him closer to his place for a beer, but that I wasn't going to go to his place to watch a movie because we don't know each other yet or have even met yet. I told him if he wanted to watch a movie then he could take me to a movie theatre though. That would have been all right.

Gary continued to argue with me asking me "Why won't you? I told you that I am a gentleman. I will certainly make you relax and be comfortable."

"Well I am sorry but I won't go back to your place."

"You know why I want to meet you, so why are you fighting this? I know that you want it to." "Want what?"

"I want to meet you for some exotic fun and to make you relax. I can do that for you. I can make you relax with a full body massage."

"Wrong. If that was what I really wanted, then I could have that by any man at anytime and anywhere. I certainly don't need to do that with you. So, now I won't meet with you on Sunday or any other day. It is quite obvious you have a one track mind, and you thought that I would go with all of this, and I won't."

"Yes you will you know that you want this."

"No I don't and I won't meet you now or ever."

"You know what Margie, you are a real whore. I can't even believe you are refusing to meet with me."

"Well believe it, and lose my phone number and my email address and do not ever call or email me again. I mean that. I won't put up with your disrespect. I have been there and done that by others, the disrespect that is. I am not that kind of lady. I don't go out with men for that reason. I am looking for a man that is looking for a long term relationship and not just sex. So have your sexual fantasies with someone else, because it certainly won't be with me."

"Sure, you will give in to me eventually. And when you do, and you will, you will wish that you had met me long ago. I can make you feel like no other man ever has or ever will now or in the future. You will see."

"I will never be with you, so you just need to leave me alone now."

I knew that he wouldn't stop, so I just hung up on him. This whole conversation with Gary is just another example of why I am getting such a bad attitude and not wanting to meet any man now. This is also the reason why I am not going to this party all dressed up and am just going the way that I normally dress. I just don't want to find men that are looking for the woman who are physically attractive and not how we are as a person inside. Society, as it is, looks at the person from the outside in, instead of the inside out.

So, I am going to this party with the idea that if a man doesn't like the way I look the day of the party compared to the last party, then they aren't worth my time. With that said I am going to this party with my hair the way it normally is and not curled or up. I am going in jeans, a nice shirt and comfortable shoes, and not a dress or a skirt and heels. I am also going with minimal makeup, only eyeliner and mascara and not all of the facial makeup to try and hide all of my wrinkles. I am not a young woman without any wrinkles, I am an older woman and as such, I won't make me out to be a younger woman. I am proud of who I am.

Margie Garrett

Everyone, including myself, can improve the quality of their lives. I am doing that in the inside and not my physical looks. I don't care anymore what the men think or want when it comes to a ladies physical appearance then I just think that they have small minds, and don't want to look behind their looks, shame on them for being the way that they are. I am certainly not saying that all of the men are that way. I know that there are good men out there somewhere. The good men, however, are very few and far between. I just hope one day, I will be lucky enough to meet one of them, but they sure are in hiding.

So, if I happen to meet a nice guy tonight, it will be because of who I am and not what I would portray if I were to dress up. Like I said before though, I am not going to impress anyone tonight, but just to have a good time. I am who I am. Like it or not. I really don't care at this time in my life. I guess, my confidence and attitude has improved, but I still have such a long way to go.

My biggest fear is approaching and talking to people that I don't know. I become very anxious. I guess I am kind of shy when it comes to that and very scared. I just can't bring myself to approaching others, at least not yet. I am so nervous what they will think.

I get to the bar early and the singles are already starting to come in. The band is now getting set up. I have made up my mind that I was going to have fun tonight and not just sit there all night with absolutely no interactions or dancing. I don't know if I can pull this off or not. I sure am going to try really hard though.

The party is now starting; the band now is playing the music. Some singles are all hyped and already out dancing on the dance floor. Some are mingling with others unlike Donna and me. That just isn't me, at least not this time. Hopefully in time I will be able to do that, but I just can't yet. I have been like this, ever since I can remember, even when I was young. Some things are hard to change, but what is the saying, oh yes it is,

"For things to change you have to change, and for things to get better you have to get better."

"I like this song Donna, let's go out and dance."

She said, "By ourselves?"

"Yes why not? I told myself I was going to have fun and dance even if the guys wanted to be some wall flowers and not ask us. Come on, let's go have some fun. Maybe if they see us out there having fun, then we might get lucky and one or more of them will ask us to dance."

"Okay, let's do it then."

And so we did. We are having a blast tonight despite the guys not approaching us at all again.

Margie Garrett

Tim showed up at the party a little after midnight. I was really surprised that he even came, to be honest. I was even more surprised with all of the beautiful woman here, that he would even notice me, let alone come over to my table to talk to me. Here he comes though.

He said, "Hey Margie, haven't talked to you in a while. I have been so busy at work. I feel like I never get any time to really relax lately, so I just thought that I would come and check out the party. So how have you been doing?"

"I am doing well, thanks for asking."

"So can I have this dance, after all I did promise you one."

"Well you don't have too; I am certainly not going to hold you to that one."

"No, really, I want to. If I didn't, I wouldn't have asked you."

"Okay."

So we went out to the dance floor and danced to a couple of songs then we went back to the table.

"So work is keeping you pretty busy?"

"Yes they are. I haven't had many days off and working long hours too."

"I wondered what happened to you, when you stopped talking to me much lately."

"Well that is why. If you will excuse me, one of my friends is over there. I am going to go over there and say hi. I will be back in a few."

It makes me really wonder how much of what he said was true. I looked over to where he went, and he was with another woman and they went out on the dance floor. I guess jealousy and confusion set in with me now, but then again we were not solely together.

So he had the right to dance and talk with whomever he chooses too. I guess I was just hoping that we had more of a relationship than just friends, but I guess I was wrong. I just am not good enough, I guess to attract the nice guys for a long term relationship. Where are they? Are they all in hiding?

Oh well, Tim never came back to my table, which is the story of my life. He probably left with the other lady. I sure was hoping that he would come back though, but he didn't. Donna and I went back out on the dance floor, when I had realized that he wasn't coming back. We left before the party ended. It wasn't too early though.

I had another message from Gary, when I had gotten home. It was a really nasty one too. He said he was never going to leave me alone. And he also called me every dirty name that you could think of. I just saved the message in a separate folder and didn't respond to it at all. I figured, I would save them all if he doesn't stop and I have to get a restraining order to keep him away from me.

I had another message from Tim asking me where I went. He had come back to the table and I was gone.

Tim called me and said "Hi Margie, what happened to you last night, I came back to your table and you were gone"

"I left early, I figured that you were with the other lady, so I left."

"I wish that you hadn't, I wanted another dance with you. So what have you been up to lately?"

"I have been looking for another place to live. This place just isn't working for me anymore. With it getting closer to the cold and winter months, I really don't want to be living here with no heat. I can't go through another winter like I did last year. It is just not going to happen."

"I don't blame you. I sure couldn't live like that. Well, are you finding anything good?"

"Actually, I did. I found a little two bedroom house on a lake in a city about a half an hour from here. It has a secluded street too. It is really pretty and nice out that way."

"Well, I am glad you found a place, when do you think that you will be moving out there?"

"I probably will in a couple of weeks. I still have to set up a time to meet with the landlord and sign the lease, and then there is the obvious packing that I have to do."

"Well, can I see you then this weekend?"

"I would like that."

"Maybe, we can watch a movie and have some popcorn."

"That sounds like a plan."

"Well, I need to get going here. I have to get something to eat and then crash, for the night. I have a very long day ahead of me. You take care okay, and I will get back with you about the day and time for this weekend.

After getting off of the phone, I was so excited that he wanted to see me again. I had to share my excitement.

So I called Donna, "Hey Donna, guess who I just got off the phone with?"

"Was it Tim from last night?"

"Yeah, it was. I didn't think that I would hear from him again, being that he was with that other woman most of last night. He wondered where I went. He said that he came back to the table and I was gone."

"Wow, you are kidding me. That is great."

"What do you think about him?"

"I think he is handsome and seems to be a good guy, but then you just never know. He seems nice enough though."

"I am so happy for you and hope your relationship with Tim builds to something really special."

"We will see, but so far he seems to be more comfortable with just hanging out at my place, and not really taking me anywhere. I don't just want to sit around here all weekends with him. His job requires him to be on the road all of the time, but ghee's you would think he would, at the very least, take me out for dinner. He isn't though, I don't expect him to spend a lot of money on me, but it sure would be nice if he thought that I was at the very least worth a drink at a local bar. Oh well, like I said, we will see how far it goes with him."

"You are right; you would think he would at least do that. He sure sounds like a cheap skate. Doesn't he? I can totally see how you would feel that way. I wonder why he doesn't. It sounds like he certainly has enough money to afford drinks for the both of you. I wonder why he is like that."

"I have no idea, but I will tell you one thing, I am not about to wait for him, or dating him exclusively. I am going to continue looking, and if one of them wants to take me out, I am certainly not going to turn them down just because I think that Tim will be coming over. Forget that. No way. I am doing that that for any guy. So how did your night go last night? Did you meet anyone?"

"No, I talked with a couple of guys, but they were obviously not interested in me. What is wrong with me Margie anyways? I don't understand why I can't get past the initial call with them. Seems that is as far as I get. I just don't get it. Can you tell me what I am doing wrong here, and why I can't get past that point?"

"I don't think that you are doing anything wrong. You just haven't found the right man that has interest in you. The men that I have found are mostly jerks who are only interested in one thing, sex. Or they think that they are all that and then some. When in reality, they are total jerks."

"Well, time is awaiting, I am not getting any younger here."

"I feel the same way that you do."

"Well, it is getting late, so I am going to have to let you go, I have to get some sleep here. I will talk to you tomorrow, okay. Bye."

"Okay, you take it easy and don't be so hard on yourself. I will be here if you need to talk. Bye for now."

"Bye."

I went back on the site and received an instant message from a guy called Mike. Turns out he is from Canada. He introduced himself and asked me a question. He asked if my profile is who I say that I am. He wanted to know how old my picture was. I told him that it was about three months old. He said that was good, because he was tired of meeting woman who had pictures on their profiles that were lies and that he was tired of meeting woman that had pictures that didn't portray themselves at all. He said that some of them say that they are fit and average woman, and it turned out that they were overweight. He also asked if my profile was true, as far as me being spontaneous. I told him that there are times when I can't sleep and that I will just get into my jeep and go driving around with absolutely no destination at all. So he said to me, so you are telling me that your profile says that you are spontaneous and you are not lying about that. I told him, that is exactly what I am saying and that I don't lie about it.

He asked me if I would come to Canada and meet with him right then and there. I told him that I would if I had the money for gas and border charges, but that if he were here, I would do just that. He said, well don't worry about that, and that he would take care of the border charges and give me some money for gas too, if I were to meet with him right then. I told him that I would then. I hope that I am not going to get myself in trouble here, and that I am not being stupid and naïve to meeting with him and being spontaneous, beings that it is late at night. I didn't think that he would try anything with me. How stupid and naïve can I be. So I did meet with him, which was a big mistake, since he did want to have sex with me. He pinned me down in my jeep and started to take advantage of me and rape me. I told him to stop it, but he wouldn't. Then he started to get violent. I was so scared that I wouldn't be able to get out of the situation, but I did. He scared me so badly. I asked him for the money to get back to the United States and home. He became very irate with me and said that he thought that I was kidding him when I told him that I didn't have the money or gas in my jeep. I told him that I really didn't. Then he was even worse and said that he didn't either and that he would have to go get some money for me.

Margie Garrett

He never came back. I waited about forty minutes for him and then realized that he wasn't coming back. I was stranded in Canada and scared. I didn't know what to do. Luckily there was a hotel next door. I went in and asked to speak with the manager. When he came to the desk I told him that I was in trouble and he stopped me and asked me if I needed money to get back to the United States. He asked if I was lured over here, and I said that I was. The manager said that he wishes that I could catch them, but he hasn't been able to stop them from luring American citizens across the border to have sex with them.

He gave me the money to get back to the United States. I received a phone call from Mike about forty five minutes later and said that he was glad that I made it back all right. I told him that I couldn't believe that he did that to me, and that he needed to delete all of his profiles from all of the dating sites, or I would have no choice but to report him to the Canadian and the United States authorities, and that I would be checking to make sure that he does just that. He said that I was bluffing and that I wouldn't do it. I told him to watch me, and that he has until I get home to do it too. I checked to make sure that he did it. He did.

I am so upset with myself right now. It is one thing to be a spontaneous person, but I was totally stupid and naïve. Seems like I am not learning what these men want all of the time. I guess that I had hoped that he would have been different, but he is just like all of the rest of the men that I have met. I am so sick of all of this dating crap. What in the world is the matter with me? Why am I so stupid? I am so depressed right now. Why I can't I learn from my past experiences? Why do I keep connecting with the wrong men? Do they think that I am that desperate to have sex? I just wish I could find a good guy, one that doesn't expect sex all of the time, and one that can accept me and respect my wishes. Be a descent and caring man. I can't find that one guy though. Why?

I am beginning to think that I will be alone for the rest of my life, so I might as well accept it. I am so depressed and upset right now, I cry myself to sleep again, seems like I do that a lot anymore. Sometimes still, I just don't want to wake up in the morning for another day of feeling so hopeless and lonely. I know that I had to leave my marriage, but I am just so lonely now. I am all alone with no one to talk to all of the time. I just can't stand this. I feel like there is no escape for me. I just want to be happy.

Margie Garrett

Now I have been diagnosed with bipolar depression, which seems to be affecting every part of my life now. I hurt with pain all of the time and I don't sleep very well either. Relationships, well that is a joke for me too. Sometimes, I wonder if there is something wrong with my health all of the time now, because of all of the pain and not being able to sleep or concentrate on anything. I feel so hopeless, and I don't feel like I am worth anything anymore. I just can't seem to get past this depression. It has been months now since I left my marriage and have been alone. I try so hard to not show my depression though with others, not in any way show how depressed, hopeless and loneliness that I feel all of the time.

Over the next couple of days I felt completely alone again, but I wasn't going to give in to these men either. I was stripped of my self-confidence so badly. Get it back totally, but I certainly am trying too. That is really all that I can do.

I am seriously getting tired of these first meets with men though. I wish that I could get just one guy that I could be with for more than one date though. The good men certainly are hard to find that is for sure. I just continue looking though. Most of the time, I just want to give up and not bother anymore. Sure don't want to be alone and so unhappy though, but the truth of the matter is, your life is what you make of it, whether I have a man in my life or not. I just feel like I may never find the right man for me though, wherever he is.

CHAPTER 9

Where Is Mr. Right?

As I continue looking, I became more and more frustrated with the male gender. Never knowing from one to the other, what they are really looking for in a relationship. Most of the men as well as woman lie on their profiles. So you just never really know until you meet with them. I just can't tell who the good guys and who are the bad ones. It is frustrating for sure. I continue on though, because they will never find me, nor will I find them if I stop looking. I just don't know where to look except for the singles parties, bars, or some of the other singles sites that there are. So I just continue what I am doing in hopes of finding him. I am so tired of the whole thing though. I just don't see this going anywhere.

As I sit here searching the profiles again,

Donna calls me and asks, "Hi Margie, how did your date go yesterday?"

"Not good, again this one turned out to be a real jerk too. All he wanted to do was get into my pants too. I am so sick and tired of meeting men these days. All I end up with is a bunch of disappointments. How about you? Have you had any luck with meetings lately?"

"Me either, my luck has been the same as yours. I met this guy a couple of days ago, but there definitely wasn't any chemistry there. He was a nice guy and everything, but was kind of boring. He did nothing for me at all. Maybe, I am just being too picky. I just don't know any more either. I just didn't feel anything for him."

"I have another date this Friday with another guy. His name is Gary. We are supposed to go out dancing at this club that has a disc jockey that plays mostly seventies disco music. It sounds like fun. We will see what happens with him. I will let you know how this one goes. I sure hope that it goes better than this last one."

"Okay, well make sure you let me know. Well I have a lot to do today, so I will let you go for now. Bye." "Okay, try to have a good day today. Bye for now."

I don't let anyone see how depressed that I really am. I cry during the day when no one is around to see me. I cry myself to sleep at night feeling so lonely and hopeless that the next day will be better than the yesterday or the past. I just feel like every day is going to get worse than the day before. The depression and fear stay in my life. I try so hard to be positive, especially when I am with someone, whether male, female, friends or family, but the positive attitude just isn't in me at all anymore.

I am now and know that I am in a major depression. I can't sleep at night. I have absolutely no appetite. I can't concentrate on anything anymore. I doubt everyone's expectations. I am tired all of the time now. And I don't care whether I live or die. I seem to be anxious about everything anymore. I know that I have to get beyond this depression, I just don't know whether I can or not. I don't want to be lonely anymore, but I want a guy that can respect me and love me for who I am and not what he wants me to be. I won't give in to their expectations of sex. I just won't. I want a true guy, a respectful guy. Why can't I find him? Where is he? Should I just give up on life? I just don't want to live anymore like this? I feel so sad, lonely and not worth anything.

Margie Garrett

Where Are You

By Margie Garrett

As I look for you
I feel so blue
In time I knew
I would find you
I look and I view
I find some new
Looking through and through
I get so blue
Tired of all the new
That seems to never come true
I never knew
If he was true
Will I ever find the one that is true?
Or will I always feel so blue
I just can't see through
The ones that are just not true
I try so hard to get through
All the times that I am so blue
I have no clue
If I will ever find you
I look, I do
But I still get so blue
Will I ever find you?
As I look through and through
As I stew and I grew
I just can't find you
Where are you?
In all of my new

I can't see through
A lot of the bad, I knew
As I grew
And I knew
I simply came to be bluer
Frustrating I knew
Where are the true?
Will I ever find you?
As I look through and through
I find a lot of new
But none that are true
I continue to look for you
I will find you, eventually I knew
My future holds the one new
That will be true
So I continue to view
Till I find the one man that is true

Margie Garrett

I woke up this morning and had decided that I was just going to take a break from all of the searching. I am tired and bored with all of it anyways, and I just don't feel that good today. My Crohn's Disease is really affecting me today and I am in a lot of pain, and the depression, really isn't helping my mood and pain either. I am just very tired today. So I am just going to try and relax and get some rest.

And so I didn't get on the computer at all today. I just didn't want to deal with any of it today. Not only was the pain bothering me, but I felt weak and dizzy today too and very lethargic. Just had absolutely no ambition or energy to do anything. I slept away most of the day. I just couldn't do anything. I sure hope that I feel better tomorrow, because I have that date with Gary. I was in a considerable amount of pain all night.

Well I have to meet with Gary today, and it was too late to cancel the date with Gary. I couldn't do that. It would be rude, and I am just not that way. So I tried all day to feel better, but I couldn't and was still in so much pain. It wasn't quite as severe as last night, but I am still hurting pretty bad.

I got myself ready and left for the club to go meet with Gary hiding my pain so that he didn't see it. I had become pretty good at hiding and dealing with the pain, because I sure didn't want it to take control of my life. I just wasn't going to let that happen or I would just roll over and be in bed on pain medication all of the time. And that just wasn't the kind of life that I wanted for myself.

I arrived on time and Gary wasn't there yet. Strike one for Gary. He didn't call me on my cell phone to let me know that he was running late either. And sitting at the club by myself, is not something that I feel comfortable doing. Gary walked in about fifteen minutes late.

I joked with him and said "Hi Gary, I thought the woman were supposed to be the ones arriving late. You are fifteen minutes late. I was beginning to think that you stood me up and was about to leave."

"Sorry, I got stuck in a traffic accident. I am glad that you didn't leave. Can I get you a drink?"

"Yes, I would like one."

I think that the whole date started on a bad note, but I stayed and we danced a few dances. He wasn't a very good dancer ever though he thought that he was. We didn't talk much at all either. I really didn't have a whole lot to say to him. I just wasn't feeling anything at all for him. Gary asked me,

"I am kind of hungry. Do you want to go get a bite to eat?"

I said, "Sure, we can do that. I am kind of hungry too."

Even though, I really wasn't hungry. I wanted to give him another try outside the dancing and see how he was at the restaurant. He was just as bad there. No, actually, he was worse than the club. Gary was nothing like I had hoped he would be. He was actually gross. Eating with him was horrible. Not only was he spitting his food when he was eating, but he took his dentures out before he started eating, disgusting to say the least. Any attraction that I may have had was sure gone now. Gary wanted to give me a kiss goodnight, I pulled away shook his hand and said

"Thank you for meeting with me."

He said, "You are welcome. I will give you a call tomorrow. Drive home safely."

I said, "I will." Gary said, "I will talk to you tomorrow. Good night."

I got into my jeep and drove away. Gary tried calling me the next day; I just ignored all future calls from Gary. He certainly wasn't Mr. Right for me, that is for sure. Depressed, disgusted, frustrated and lonely, that is how I feel right now. I am so close to giving up and resigning to the fact that I will never find a man, and that I will be alone for the rest of my life. So I better find happiness somewhere else in my life just in case I don't. I am tired of looking now. I still do though, I have absolutely no idea why I even bother, accept for the fact that I don't want to be alone.

After a couple of days of Gary trying to reach me, he finally gave up. I figured if I didn't answer his calls and just ignored them, that he would eventually get the hint. There just wasn't anything there with him. He was just totally disgusting. I sure couldn't kiss him. Gross.

After a couple of days of Gary trying to reach me, he finally gave up. I figured if I didn't answer his calls and just ignored them, that he would eventually get the hint. There just wasn't anything there with him. He was just totally disgusting. I sure couldn't kiss him. Gross.

"I am thinking about going. Not sure if I have to work that night though. I hope not, because I would really like to go meet this one guy that will be there. I have been talking to him for a few days and now he seems nice. I hope I don't have to work that night."

"Why haven't you set up a meet outside the party?"

"I just feel more comfortable meeting him there. Then there is no real commitment to stay with him all night if it doesn't work out with us."

"Yeah, I can totally understand, after my last date. I am thinking about hosting some parties. I haven't decided whether I want to yet, but I am sick of all these meets I have and this would be a good way of meeting more men in one night, and then I won't have to do the single meets. I sure am thinking about doing them though."

"That would be cool. Where do you think you would do them, and how often will you have them?"

Margie Garrett

"I am not sure yet, but if I do, I will probably have them twice a month, one on the east side and the other on the west side."

"Well, I will for sure go. Just let me know."

"I will be posting it on the site if and when I do."

"Cool, well time to get ready for work. I will talk to you later. Bye."

"Bye Donna."

CHAPTER 10

Raped and Scared

I went online again in the singles site, just to check messages. I have no clue why I continue too, but I do. All I am attracting anyway are the wrong men, but I keep trying. I have a couple of new messages. I haven't talked with these men before though. I can only hope that they will be nice and not anymore self-centered jerks that only want a one night stand with me, which they will never get anyways. We will see though.

So I started to talk to Dan, which was one of them. And over the next couple of days.

He finally asked me, "So Margie, would you want to meet me for a drink tomorrow?"

"Yes, I would like that, where would you like to meet?"

"Do you know the sports bar that is over on Fifteenth Street?"

"Yes, I do."

"Would you like to meet me there about four o'clock tomorrow afternoon?"

"Okay, that sounds good."

"Okay, I will see you tomorrow then."

"Okay, I will see you then. Bye."

Margie Garrett

Here I go again; I must be out of my mind meeting yet another man. How is this one going to be? I am not getting my hopes up though, because to be honest, I expect Dan will be about the same as all of the others, but I said that I would meet him, so I will.

As I am driving to the sports bar, I get this really weird feeling. I don't know why or what it meant. I probably should just turn around and go back home, but I didn't listen to my feelings. I went ahead and arrived there. I went into the sports bar. Dan was sitting at the bar. He looks like he has been here for a while, and had already had a few to many drinks. The way he was sitting there, his shirt half out of his pants and just his demeanor.

Me and my darn respect for others, does nothing but get me into trouble. Why, I decided to even go over to him is beyond me. I have to be crazy. So I go up to the bar and sit next to him.

I said, "Hi Dan, I am Margie."

"Hey, how are you?"

"Good thanks. So how long have you been here?"

"I have been here probably about an hour or so."

The bartender came over and asked me, "What can I get for you?"

"A Bud Light would be good."

Dan said to me, "I am getting a little hungry, did you want to get some appetizers to eat."

He didn't ask me what I wanted he just called the bartender over and said that he wanted the mix appetizer plate. The bartender said to him that it would be up in a few minutes. The bartender brought my beer over to me and said that it would be three dollars. I looked over at Dan, and he just looked away from me, as if to say that he had no intentions of paying anything for me. So I had to pay for my own drink.

He really didn't have a whole lot to say to me either. And what he is saying is with slurred words like he is drunk and has had way too many drinks already. Before the appetizers came he ordered yet another beer which was brought out with the appetizers. The bartender came back with them and had said that it will be twelve dollars and ninety five cents. Once again, Dan didn't pay for those either. What a date this is turning out to be. I am paying for the whole bill.

With tips and all, I had to put out around twenty dollars that I should have never had to pay. I was so disgusted with him that I didn't even want to stay and finish the appetizers. So I just told Dan, "Well, this has been swell, but I think that I am just going to go now." So I just got up and started to walk out. Dan gets up and says that he will walk me to my car. I told him that it was ok and that he really didn't need too, and that I can find my own car. It is not like it is dark or anything. He said that he wanted to though.

Margie Garrett

He is now totally freaking me out. I didn't know what to do. It was daylight though and there were people coming in and out of the bar. So I figured that I would be all right. So I get to my jeep, and Dan is right behind me. I turned around and said to him that I will see him later. He goes to give me a kiss. He was so close to me. I didn't think he could get much closer. He did though. I turned my cheek so that he couldn't kiss me. I can smell the liquor all over him. He just plain reeked of alcohol. He pushed himself even closer to me. I told him again that I had to go. Dan asked me why I wouldn't even kiss him. I told him that I just don't kiss on the first meets. He said that he is the exception to my rules. I said that he is not and that I just don't. He said that I at least owed him that. I said that I did not owe him anything and to please just leave me alone. I tried to get into my jeep, but I couldn't. Dan pushed me right up against the door and started kissing me on my neck, because I turned my face. He had pinned me so tight that I couldn't move. He took my arms both and pulled them above my head. He held them with his one hand as he used his other hand to go down my shirt and fondle my breasts.

I told Dan, "Dan stop it and let me go. I will scream".

He said to me, "No, you won't."

"Please Dan, stop it, stop it."

"You like this and you know it."

He was so close to me and had me pinned so tightly that I couldn't move. There was no one in the parking lot that I could even scream to for help and he knew it. He is so strong. I can't break away from him.

I said to him, "Dan, please stop it, please."

"You love being touched by me. I know that you do you slut. You want it, you know that you do. Say it."

"No I don't."

"Say it."

"No I won't, because I don't want it."

"Sure you do."

Margie Garrett

Dan went even further; he then pushed himself even closer, so no one could see what he was going to do to me. He then took his hand out of my shirt. I had a skirt on for the date. He then took that hand and lifted up my shirt far enough for him to put his hand down my skirt and into my underwear. As he did that, I was so scared. It was almost like I was paralyzed. I was so afraid that I just let him, because I was afraid that he would hurt me. I had to wait until he pulled away from me far enough that I could stop him.

I am so afraid that he is going to rape me tonight. I am so scared. I am crying.

Dan said to me, "Shut up and stop your crying. I said that you owe me and I am going to collect now, so just shut up."

"Dan please stop it, I won't tell anyone. I know it is because you have had too much to drink. If you let me go, I promise that I won't tell anyone. Really I promise."

"Shut up and just enjoy this. You know you like it, so why the act?"

"Dan you are scaring me. I am not acting here."

"Shut up or I am going to tape your mouth you slut. Quit fighting me."

"No, No, please stop, please."

I had to just let him do whatever he wanted so that he wouldn't hurt me until he pulled away from me. I am so scared. How am I going to get away? Dan wasn't breaking away or stopping at all. He still had his hand on my arm pinned above my head. He continued kissing my neck, and then put his face down my shirt and started licking me down there. I continued silently crying. Tears are just pouring out of my eyes. When he did that though, he had pulled away just enough that he could get his tongue further down my shirt. I have to think how I can break free from him. He is so strong, and has me pinned so tight. He isn't stopping though.

I know that I have to do something to get free from him. I just let him believe that I wouldn't fight him anymore, in hope that he will let loose just enough. Let's face it, what else could I do. I just remembered what I had learned about rape. They say to not fight it, just let it happen to save your life; until you know that you can break free. He then took his hand out of my shirt and back up to help hold both arms again. I should have done something then, but I didn't have enough time too. I didn't think fast enough. Dan started kissing my face this time. I tried turning my face, but it wasn't working. He was then, at that time, so hard and turned on; he pushed himself all the way onto me, rubbing up and down against me. Now, I am seriously afraid. What is he going to do to me now?

There was a field not far from my jeep where I was parked. The weeds were very high. He then grabbed me, put the tape over my mouth and pulled me away from my jeep before anyone else came to the sports bar, or come out of it. He took me way into the middle of the field, and pushed me down on the ground. He then took my underwear off. He lay right on top of me kissing my breasts and raping me. At that point, I now can't do anything I just lay there paralyzed.

He got away with raping me. I am so sick. I am just so sick. After he was done, he just got up and walked away. I stayed in the field for a while scared and humiliated, that there was nothing that I could do to break away. Maybe what had happened was my entire fault. What is the matter with me? I hate myself for letting this happen. Why do things like this happen to me? After this, I won't meet any guy under these circumstances again, ever again. From now on, someone that I know will know who I am with that night, and where I am going. We will check in with each other every hour or so. If I don't answer the phone, then they will know that I need help. I am just not going to put myself in a vulnerable position like this again. I just can't do that anymore for my own safety.

I don't even know why I am even thinking that I would even want to meet another man after tonight. Men make me sick. Most of them, at least the ones that I have met, are either controlling, sex maniacs or pigs. I just don't think that I will ever meet a good guy. It is not like I haven't been trying. Now, every time I go to meet one, I will constantly have that fear hanging over me. I just don't know if I can do this anymore. I just have no trust in men at all now. Like I have said before, dating sure isn't the same as it was years ago.

Tonight I lay awake crying all night that I had been violated yet again by another man. I can't seem to stop crying. I sit in the bathtub scrubbing myself, so hard that my skin is red, and just trying to get him and his smell off of me. Seems that no matter how hard I try to scrub it off, just isn't enough.

It is around eight o'clock, and my phone rings, it is Donna. I just let it go to voicemail. I couldn't talk to anyone. I just can't. She left me a message asking me how my date went today. There is just no way that I can talk to anyone right now.

I became very numb now, staring off into space. I feel so empty, almost like he stripped me of any hope with a good man. I don't know how long it will be before I can even talk to anyone or even step outside these four walls. I am so alone, empty, humiliated and now scared of everyone and everything. What am I going to do? How am I going to get past this? I just don't know.

I finally cried myself to sleep. When, I awoke the next morning. I didn't feel any different. I feel just alone and scared as I did yesterday. I had another phone call last night. I didn't even hear the phone ring. It was Donna calling again. This time she had pleaded with me on voicemail, to call her back and that she was worried about me.

I still just couldn't talk to anyone. Not even Donna. I was too embarrassed. I know that she is my best friend and we have always been there for each other, but this is different. Besides, even if I did call her back, I wouldn't really be able to talk to her, because I would just break down crying again. So instead of calling her back, I wrote her a message online and didn't tell her much, except that the date was horrible and that I just am not in a position to talk about it right now.

Donna knew me well enough to know that the message was too vague and that something was seriously wrong. Something definitely happened last night so terrible that it prevented me from talking to anyone.

Will I ever feel safe enough to date a man again? I just don't know. Dan sure broke me down.

I went and took another shower. I just couldn't seem to take enough of them, not that they did me any good. Because, the truth of the matter is, it doesn't really matter how many showers I take, the showers are not going to wash away what he did to me, or the fear that I now have with me. This feeling of helplessness will never go away. It will always follow me now. Nothing that anyone can say or do for me is going to help me now. The only one that can help me now is me. I have to pull myself out of this depressed and scared state that I am in. I have to.

All that I did was crying all day again. I just couldn't stop thinking about what he did to me; and thinking if there was anything different that I could have or should have done differently. There really wasn't though. I did what I had to do. Thinking that still didn't help how I feel.

I lay here crying, the phone rings. It is Donna. She said that she is going to continue calling until I answer, because she is now really worried about me. So I did call her back, trying so hard to pull myself together enough to talk to her, without breaking down in tears crying on the phone. Donna said, "Margie, are you okay?" I said to her, "No I am not actually. I am so sorry that I haven't answered your calls. I just couldn't talk to anyone right now." "What in the world happened to you the other day? What did he do to you?"

I just started crying again, and just couldn't really talk about it. Donna knew at that point, that something was seriously wrong, and that Dan had done something seriously wrong with me Donna said, "I will be right there Margie." Donna must have known that there something seriously wrong. Dan must have done something to hurt her. Donna said, "I will be right there Margie." Donna was here within thirty minutes or so.

Donna must have known that I wouldn't answer the door, so as she walked inside she said to me,

"It is okay Margie, it is me Donna."

I couldn't even move. Donna found me on the chair in the other room all curled up in the chair and crying.

She came over and put her arms around me and said, "Oh My God Margie, I am so sorry. What happened? Can you talk to me about it?"

I was crying so hard that I couldn't talk. Donna stayed here with me. She said she wasn't going to leave me like this. She called into work, and explained that she had a family emergency and needed the day off. I sure wasn't going to fight her on it. So she stayed with me tonight, just holding me and trying to comfort me until I could stop crying enough to go to sleep. She stayed with me all night and stayed awake to help me through tonight. When I woke up the next morning, Donna was still holding me.

She said to me, "Margie, can you talk to me about what happened. What did Dan do to you the other day?"

"I went and met him at the sports bar. Dan had already had a few drinks before I even got there. Donna I had a weird feeling on the way there, but I didn't trust my own instincts and I went anyways."

I started crying again as I told Donna, "He raped me in the field next to the bar. He raped me Donna. I couldn't break away from him. I just laid there like I was paralyzed. I just couldn't move. I did nothing. I did nothing to stop him. What is the matter with me anyways?"

"There is nothing wrong with you Margie. You did what you had to do to survive." "I know, but I feel so dirty. I have showered and showered and about scrubbed myself raw, but I still feel dirty. How can I live with this feeling? I just wanted to die yesterday."

"It is going to take time for you to get through this ordeal, but you are one strong woman, and I know that you will. You will learn from this and be safer now than you ever were before, so that you can be prepared in case you are ever put in this kind of situation again. You will, Margie, it is just going to take some time before you feel comfortable enough to venture out. You will though. Right now, you just need to concentrate on healing. It is just going to take some more time. Just remember that I am here for you and always will be to help you in any way that I can."

"I know you are Donna. You are a good friend. You are like a sister to me. I am so glad that I have you in my life."

"Awe, thank you Margie. I consider you like a sister to me too. Just remember when you ever need to talk or are just feeling down to please call me. Please promise to me that you will."

"I will, I promise."

"Are you going to be okay tonight or would you like me to stay over again?"

"I will be fine Donna. Thank you so much for being here with me when I needed someone to help me to understand that I did nothing to be embarrassed or ashamed of, and that what happened was not my fault. Thank you so much, for everything."

"There is no need to thank me. That is what friends are for. To be there for each other and help each other when we need help. I will always be here for you. I hope that you know that."

"I know you will."

"Well, I need to go get a few things from the grocery store. Do you need anything?"

"No, I am fine. Besides, I am really not up for eating anything these days."

"Well you need to start eating you know. Otherwise, you will get weak."

"I know maybe I will just have some soup tonight."

"Okay, well please call me if you need anything or just want to talk. I will check in on you later. Just please remember what I said. You did nothing wrong."

"Okay, I will."

"Okay, you try and get some rest now. Bye."

"Bye Donna."

As soon as Donna walked out that door, I felt so alone again. My life felt so dark, a lot like the way that I felt before. I keep asking myself, what I am going to do. I can't and won't let that moron Dan, feel that he has won. I do regret the fact that I didn't report that he had raped me though. I can still report him, but I had scrubbed away all of the evidence. I haven't washed the clothes though, the clothes that I had on, the night of the rape. However, I didn't even know the guys last name either. He seems to be a regular at the bar though. So I might be able to find out there. Do I really want to do this though? Or do I just want to let it go. If I do that though, he will just continue like nothing is wrong and rape another one of his dates just like he did me. I just couldn't live with myself if I let that happen.

Margie Garrett

I called Donna and talked with her about what I wanted to do.

I asked "Donna will you go back with me to the bar, I want to ask the bartender if he knows this guy's last name. I just don't feel safe enough to go do this myself."

Donna said, "Of course, when did you want to go?"

"Well as soon as you can go. I just don't want to wait too much longer to report him. If they don't know though, I will just print out a copy of his profile and picture and take that to the authorities."

"Well, to be honest, I just think you shouldn't go back there, especially if he is a regular there. You don't want to confront him."

"I don't know, as much as I don't want him to get away with what he did to me, I don't know if I can go through with this either. A part of me tells me to and the other parts says to just let it go."

"Do you really think you can do that though Margie? Can you just let it go"

"I don't know. I just don't know."

"Well, why don't you think about it a make sure that is what you really want to do. In the meantime, put all of the clothes you wore that night in a sealed bag."

"Good idea, I will do that. Well I am going to try and get some sleep, so I will talk to you tomorrow. Good night Donna."

"Good night Margie. Take care."

So, over the next few days, I just sheltered myself in my home. Not going outside at all. Crying every day, and trying to decide what to do. I know that I don't want to be responsible for Dan hurting, yet another woman like he did me. I really just don't know if I can do this though. I don't want to talk to anyone about what happened, what he did and how and where he did it. I didn't and couldn't even tell Donna all of the horror of what happened to me that night. I just couldn't tell her. I am so glad that she didn't push me to let it out and to tell her. To tell anyone including the authorities will be like reliving the whole night and the horror of what Dan did to me all over again. If I do tell the authorities, and Dan is arrested for assault and rape, the all of this continues. I will have to go through all the court hearings, and then everyone would know what happened to me. People are mostly judgmental and may or may not believe me because I had no physical injuries. So some people would not even believe that had happened to me. Or could think that it was my entire fault, and they would think or could think that I asked for it. I am just torn between doing what is the right thing to do, and protecting myself from all the future ridicule I could get from people. Seems like, I can't really win either way.

As I lay awake every night crying, I can't seem to get any of this off of my mind. I just keep reliving it.

I get a phone call from Donna, "Hi Margie, are you doing any better today?"

"Not really, I just don't really know what to do."

"Well Margie, you need to do what is best for you and forget about what anyone else thinks. Besides, unless you told anyone else what had happened with Dan, the only ones that would know would be the three of us. I doubt very much that Dan will tell anyone what he had done. What you have told me or what you tell me now, will always stay between the two of us unless you say otherwise. I hope that you know that."

"I do Donna, thanks."

"You know that you have time to think about reporting this, so just take your time and heal a little more first before you commit yourself for what you could face with a nasty trial."

"I know that it will be. The whole think is scary for me. I am just not ready to even make the decision yet. I am still hurting. I put all of the clothes in a sealed bag like you had said. I put the bag into the other bedroom closet away from anywhere that I can see them. Did I tell you that I almost burned them out of disgust and pain?"

"No, you didn't tell me that. I am glad that you took my advice. It is the best thing for now. Are you taking care of yourself? Have you been eating anything?"

"I am not eating much, just little nibbles of some fruit. I just don't have any appetite. I have been mostly wasting away the last couple of days either staring or crying. I don't go on the computer, and the only one that I have talked to is you. I just don't want to be bothered by anyone else. Otherwise, I will just start crying again, and I do enough of that. I just don't want anyone else to see the pain that I am in."

"I understand, but you need to at least start eating or you will become sick. You don't want your Crohn's Disease to take over from all of the pain and stress you are under, or you will become starved and dehydrated again and end up back in the hospital. So please try to eat even if it is a small meal several times throughout the day for me. Will you do that?"

"Ok, I promise, I will try to." "Just remember, that some time will eventually heal the wounds that you have. I know that is hard to believe right now, but it really is true. You will get through this. I know that the strength you have always had in your life is what will help you."

"I sure hope that you are right. Right now, all I feel is hopelessness. Sure not feeling strong right now at all."

"You will feel it soon and you will be stronger than ever, trust me."

"I sure hope so. Well, I am going to go Donna; I just don't want to talk anymore right now. I hope that you understand. I will talk to you later."

"Okay, but if you want to talk later, please call me. You try and feel better. Bye." "Bye."

Margie Garrett

I have pretty much isolated myself for a few days now with the exception of talking to Donna. I know that I need to move on with my life. How can I do that though with what has happened? I certainly will never be able to forget. And the mere thought of meeting another man is almost impossible for me now. I can't trust any of them. I know that I need to start leaving this house and go for a walk; or to the store or just take a drive. I need to try and get my life back, instead of staying my room and crying all of the time. That behavior isn't helping me heal. Instead, it is hindering me. So tomorrow, I am going to try very hard to try and move on. I have to if I ever want anything to change.

So I crash for the night in hopes that tomorrow will be a better day. It is morning, I slept fairly well. I think that I have shed all of the tears that I can shed. As I sit here with my morning coffee, I am thinking of what I will do today different from the last several days. I know this will be a very difficult day. I have to make an effort though.

So this afternoon, I just took a drive to the park. While there, I took a walk to help clear my head of everything and to just feel the air and see all of the beautiful scenery. I decided to take a nice long scenic drive up the coast. I was gone for several hours this afternoon. To be honest, it really felt good to do it. Still not talking to anyone or going on my computer though. I am just not ready for that yet. Maybe tomorrow I will be able to do a little more and each day after until I get back to an almost normal life.

My life will never be the same as it used to be though. Dan sure changed all of that for me. I sure hope he is happy with himself. I wonder what he sees when he looks in his mirror. Or what he thinks about how he hurt me. I don't know how he can even live with himself. I sure couldn't, if I had done something like that to someone. I can't think about this now. I just have to focus on my future and how I am going to live from day to day now. I have to try and not bring it up anymore, and leave all of it in the past, if I want any kind of a future.

Each day now, I am doing a little more and venturing out a little further than the last. Finally, I am slowly getting my strength back. I feel a little better each day.

Margie Garrett

It has now been two weeks since the rape. I absolutely am not going to talk about it at all. I don't want to think about it anymore, because I realize it just brings me down again. So, I am moving on. In order to prepare myself for any future dates, I am going to the store to get some kind of a keychain or something that I can attach to a keychain to hold a trial hair spray. Why hairspray? You ask. Well, because I will be spraying it in the man's eyes, if a man ever comes close to threatening my life again. I have to protect myself from now on, and quit being so naïve and trusting.

It is Friday evening, and I know that Donna will be home from work now.

I called her, "Hi Donna."

"Hi Margie, you are sounding a lot better today."

"I am, I have spent the last couple of days driving and going for long walks to clear my head. I couldn't stay cooped up in this house anymore. What are you doing tonight? Do you have any plans?"

"Not really, I was just going to sit around here and chill. Why do you ask?"

"You want to go get a drink or something. I think I want to get out and be surrounded by others tonight and see how I will do, and I wanted to know if you would go with me. If you don't feel up to it though, it is okay."

"Wow, you really want to take a giant leap like this so soon?"

"Well, if I don't soon, I may never get the courage to ever do it again."

"Okay, well give me about an hour to get ready and I will come and pick you up."

"Great, know it is soon, but I need to do this for me."

"I will see you in about an hour then. Bye."

"See you then."

I wasn't dressing up tonight, because I just wanted to be comfortable. I wore jeans and a nice shirt, shoes, but no high heels and I didn't curl my hair either. As you can see, I wasn't going to try and hook up with a guy. I was going to just hang out with a friend and that was all for now. The place was packed. No one bothered me tonight. Everything was fine. We had a couple of beers and then left. I was okay. I didn't have any problems with being there. Donna being with me helped a lot though.

So, now that I am home, and Donna is gone, I now went a step further, I booted up my computer. I went to check my messages, which I hadn't checked in several days now, on the dating site. I wasn't too sure about answering any of them though, because now none of them can be trusted by me. If they want to date me, they will have to earn my trust.

I have my walls up now so high to protect myself. I will not put myself in any danger. The only place I meet any of them now will be at a singles party where I am surrounded by a lot of friends. If they don't want to meet there, then we just won't be meeting.

I have been meeting too many dangerous men and so far have been lucky enough to still be alive. I have been stalked, physically hit, verbally abused, harassed and now raped, all on first meets. Do you see now why I am being extremely careful? Well, that is why. I am just not going to take any more chances. I don't care how convincing they are about being good men. The others told me that to, and look at what my trust got me. Just to be hurt over and over again. That is my decision whether the men like it or not. I don't care how they feel about it.

I have about ten messages and none of the men look interesting enough to meet with them based on their profiles. Looks are not as important to me as the kind of man he really is. Looks are only skin deep. Dan was a very handsome man and look what happened with him. I answered a couple of the messages tonight and told them if they wanted to meet me, I would be most likely going to be at the party next Saturday. John answered me back and asked me to meet him sooner because of his work schedule; he probably won't be able to go to the party. I answered back, pretty much apologizing, but had told him due to recent and very dangerous first meet experiences, this is the only way that I will meet any men now. I just can't do it. John said he was sorry to hear that, and that he totally understands. He said that he will try hard to get out of work early enough that he can meet me.

So over this next week, before the party, I continue answering my messages and checking the party forum to see who has signed up to go. I added myself to that list too. There are at least two guys that messaged me that are signed up to go. They both messaged me after they noticed that I had decided to go, and asked me to save a dance for them. I am very nervous about going, but I am not going to let Dan win. It just isn't going to happen. I just hope that he doesn't show up there. If he does though, I will just go get the bouncer at the bar to kick him out. I am not going to be hurt by him again. So Donna came and picked me up so that we could go together to the party. I didn't dress up or anything. I wasn't into impressing any guy yet. I just went to be with some friends and have a good time. If the guy's ask me to dance, I will, but not expecting that to happen anyways. At this point, I don't care one way or the other, whether I get asked or not. Some might think that I am acting cold, but then they don't know everything. I just have the walls up again.

Margie Garrett

So we arrive a little early to get a table like we had done before. Around eight o'clock the place had started to get really crowded. It looks like they are putting on a great party like they always have. By nine o'clock, the place was completely full. There were no tables left and no stools at the bar. It was standing room only from then on. I, for the most part, just sat and watched everyone. I am not one to mix and mingle with others. Doing that has never been easy for me. A couple of guys tonight asked me for a dance. I did dance with them one dance and then they just moved on to the next. I went back to sit at my table with Donna.

The band was really good. So, if nothing else, I just enjoyed getting out and listening to them. Well, it was the last song of the night, so we left so we could avoid the crowd. I didn't meet any men really, the couple of dances that I did have were nice though.

Ultimate Danger

I am such a dreamer
Always a fighter
Living for the greater
Trying to avoid the baiter

I think I met the gender
Who would be so tender?
Felt my life was brighter
As I felt so much laughter

I feel I have a future
I became so much bolder
Until I met the boozer
Who became so much drunker?

Now I am falling faster
I now feel so much terror
As situation became much tougher
I now need be a fighter

I wish I had a helper
Where are you Mother?
I need to be calmer
That I can become safer
Escaping from this monster

Margie Garrett

I fear I have met a raper
Pushing his hands on my shoulders
I feel so much weaker
He is so much stronger

Full of so much anger
He pinned me in a corner
As he now became a beater
I became the screamer

I am not very clever
How do I escape this terror?
I now became a crier
I scream and scream for a helper

I sink now further and further
As I feel like such a failure
Life seems so much darker
While in so much danger

My dreams have now slipped further
As I am now in capture
Fighting from the raper
And away from the terror

I now need be braver
And think more clearly
Not wanting it rougher
Yes I am now a crier

He made me feel cheaper
As he made me his hooker
Will he kill me I wonder?
Or is he just a raper

He pushed me in the center
Of the big and high pasture
Making me his stripper
I feel so much danger

He felt so much pleasure
All I felt was horror
I am now full of anger
Because I was not the wiser

Margie Garrett

As he pins me even harder
And in me so much deeper
Will he ever be over?
Will I ever be safer?

I am away from loser
The drunker
The monster
The raper

I go home to shelter
Where I thought I could feel safer
Instead I am paler
And oh so much weaker

I get into hot water
To scour away his odor
As I scrub and scrub and lather
And use a very strong cleanser

I don't feel any better
Nor do I feel safer
Just wiser and clearer about danger
I can only pray I will again be a dreamer
And not fear all of the danger

CHAPTER 11

Friends of a Life Time

I haven't met many friends before and after my divorce. I have a really hard time making friends. It isn't that I don't want them, it is just that I feel totally uncomfortable talking to new people that I don't know. A lot of my friends are online. Some of them I have personally met and spent time with, and the others I continue talking to online or by email, text messages or by phone. One of the men that I had met online turned out to be a very supportive friend, helping me in a time of need, and when I was in a difficult time in my life. His name is Jon. Jon is one of those men that fit into what I think is the one percent of the male population considered to be the good guys. He is truly a one of a kind friend, one that will and has always been here for me when I needed to talk to and confide in someone. I am truly honored to have him as a friend. No matter what my problems were, I could always count Jon to be right there to help me get through them.

Margie Garrett

Friends, true friends that is, are really hard to find. When I find them, I certainly hope that I can keep them, even my online friend, ones that I have been able to meet or the ones that I just confide in online. I consider all of them awesome friends. Jon is an absolutely incredible musician. He is an Acoustic Folk Rock musician. He performs in many cities surrounding the Metro area as well as other cities. I have only had a couple of opportunities to see him perform due to schedules. I am hoping that, in the future, I will be able to make it to a lot of his upcoming performances throughout the Michigan area.

The other close important friend that I have, of course, is Donna. She too helps me get through all of my life experiences. She is such an inspiration to me too, one, that gives me such good advice when I need it so desperately. She has helped me out so much with so many things that have been awful experiences in my life. She has also been there to enjoy some of the good things that have happened to me. She is definitely like a sister to me, She is one loving and very caring friend that I am honored to have as a true friend too. She is even more so than Jon, I was able to confide in about the rape that I had gone through. I love her so much for being there and staying with me and helping me get through such an awfully horrible night that I had after the rape

I had always hoped that I would be able to find two of the best friends that I could ever have. I am so honored. I feel like they are family to me. These two friends always walk beside me no matter what my problems seem to be. They are truly my rock. I can always count on the both of them when I need them. It seems like I never seem to say anything, in order for these two friends of mine, to know that I need help or just to talk too. They both make me feel that I never have to explain anything to them. I just feel with them, that I never have to feel like I need to be strong to have them in my life. They never ask me if I need anything, they just do it, just like Donna had come right over and spent the night with me when I desperately needed a friend that night. I was and am so grateful to her for caring and loving me that much to come right over and watch over me that night.

As far as Jon, we might not see or talk as much as I talk to Donna, but he is always there online to talk to me and help me with his intelligent sight on certain situations with men and what the expectations are. They both are genuinely caring friends.

I just feel like there is nothing in this world that I could possibly do that would damage the friendship that I have with Donna and Jon, nothing at all. At least I feel that, and I can only hope that we will be true friends forever. I sure don't ever want to lose their friendship. I care about the two of them so much. I would do anything for either one of them if they ever needed me too.

Donna and Jon both believed in me and expressed to me what a strong woman I am, even when I doubted myself. I just never thought of myself that way. They love me just the way that I am, and have absolutely no expectations from me.

I know that when I am so depressed and I feel so down and lonely, I always think of my two best friends with a smile, because I know that they will always be around for me.

Donna has always had a way of giving me the support and encouragement to do things that I seriously did not think that I could ever do. She has such faith in me, as does Jon. They never judge me for the things that have gone bad in my life either.

I have had many friends, but none have stayed when I began to have problems in my life. I thought they too, were true friends, but I was so wrong. I had several friends before the divorce who are now gone. I don't know what I did or said to them, but truth is, I guess they were only acquaintances and not true friends at all. Donna and Jon both seem to bring out the best in me and always have.

I asked Donna about hosting some singles parties. It looks like she might have to be there for me again with these upcoming parties, to give me the strength and encouragement that I need to be able to overcome this obstacle in my life. I can't wait to get her opinions later on how to do them and where to have them. I hope that Jon too will be able to come and check them out. These are true friends that will be with me forever.

CHAPTER 12

Hosting Singles Parties

After these last few days, of feeling so alone, with nothing to look forward to and no excitement in my life. I knew that I had to do something to change my life around. There is another party coming up in a couple of days. I decided to go. This time though, I am going to dress up a little more than the last. Look a little better and see what happens this time.

Eventually things have to turn around for me. I know that. I am shy and very reserved, but I have to work on my fears and all of the insecurities that I have when it comes to meeting new people. It sure isn't an easy thing for me to overcome. So how am I going to get through all of this? The only answer that I have is to keep trying. It will happen, it has to happen. I sure don't want to be alone for the rest of my life. I deserve some happiness. Don't I? Doesn't everyone?

So the party is tomorrow night. What am I going to wear? I have a nice blue pair of jeans and a nice low cut black shirt. I think that I am just going to wear that. I am really not into heels, but am going to make an exception and wear my blue jean heels. I have black earrings to go with my black necklace. I am going to do a French manicure and pedicure and curl my hair this time too. I am going to the salon to have a French manicure and pedicure. I will do my hair too. I am going to the salon to have a makeover and they will do my hair there too.

Margie Garrett

I had met a few people at the last couple of parties that I had sat with. They are all very nice. I am sure that they will be at the party again this time. I am sure that they will let us sit at their table again, or at least I hope that they will.

Well, today is the day. I am considering this day the beginning of my future. I sure hope that I can at least turn a couple of heads tonight. I sure don't hold my breath on it though. Let's face it; I am sure not beautiful, like some of these women are. I don't even remotely come close to them. I am just me though, and I am sure not going to portray someone that I am not.

Here goes nothing, I am here at the bar, and they are all here. I am a nervous wreck. I walk up to their table and said Hi to all of them. All said hi back to me. Talk about awkward. I didn't know what else to say and they are all very nice and asked me if I wanted to sit at their table with them. So I did.

As I had predicted though, this party was just like all of the others. I had fun hanging with them, but I certainly didn't turn any heads tonight. Oh well. Guess I can just consider it one step toward my future. If nothing else, I watched the host and hostess work the crowd tonight and observed how they do these parties, and just see what is all involved in hosting them. I think that I should just watch them over the next couple of parties and see how they do things. Then think about whether I would like to host some myself. I don't know if I am up for taking something like that on or if I can even do it. All I do know is that I have to get better with all of this or I am never going to find a man.

It was beginning to be a little easier going to them knowing them guys and being able to hang out with them. I hope that I can be a close friend of theirs. I really like all of them.

The parties are great, but they are only held in the area once a month, so if I want to go to the other, I would have to go downriver to the other one. Which would probably be good for me, because I could meet some new people there too? There is a party there next week. Maybe, I will go to that one. Sure might be different than these.

Margie Garrett

Well, I am beat and think that I am going to get some rest. As I wake up the next morning, I am thinking of what I will do today to pass the time. I am not feeling much like doing anything today. My Crohn's Disease is acting up again this morning. I can see that with the way that I am feeling, I won't be doing anything. I am too cramped up this morning. I really hate being in pain. All of the time, I never knew, from one day to the next, how I will feel. All that I know is that today is one of those days that I can't hide my pain from anyone. So I don't want to see anyone today, because there is just no way of hiding how I am feeling. When I am like this, I spend the day either in bed or curled up on the couch with a pillow pushing up against my stomach, because of the pain. I feel absolutely horrible today.

The phone is ringing, it is Donna. I can't talk right now, so I let it go to voicemail. I will try and call her back later. I am going back to bed after I take something for the pain. I sure hope that it helps me. Sometimes they do, but most of the time the pain is just too severe.

As I wake up the next morning, after a night of pain, it isn't looking good for me today either. I just can't stand this pain. I wish that I had something to just knock me out. After a couple of hours of tossing and turning, I finally fell asleep for a while after taking a pain pill. When I woke up several hours later, I was still no better than I was before. I went back and lay down again. I am in tears right now. I live each and every day praying for at least one pain free day and night, but it has never come yet. This disease is horrible. Living like this is so hard. It is a challenge every single day now.

None of my friends even know about my Crohn's and I really want to keep it that way. That is why it was hard for me to not answer the phone and tell Donna this morning. I just don't want anyone to know. I haven't even gone online today. I just can't seem to do anything.

Donna is calling me again. "Hi Donna, I am sorry that I didn't call you back."

"Hi Margie, are you okay?"

"Not really, haven't felt good today."

"Do you have the flu or something?"

"I don't know." I couldn't bring myself to telling her yet what is really affecting me.

Margie Garrett

"Well I hope that you feel better soon."

"I sure hope so too. I have been in bed all day today."

"Well you go get some rest and I will check in with you tomorrow."

"Okay, thanks Donna. Bye."

"Bye for now."

So I went back to bed again. I had exchanged my phone number with a couple of friends that I sat with at the party the other night, and I received another call. This one was from Janet.

She said, "Hi Margie, how are you?"

"I am okay and yourself?"

Yes, I know, you are thinking why I had told Janet that I was okay. Well, like I said, I don't really know her well enough to let her know how I really am. I think that Donna suspects something is wrong, but just isn't pushing me to find out what yet.

Janet said, "I am good, it was nice seeing you the other night. You looked really nice."

"Thanks, you did too."

"So I wanted to ask you if you wanted to go with us to the downriver party this weekend."

"Yes, I am glad that you asked me, because I do want to go, but don't really know anyone there. So it will be great to go with you. Thanks for asking me."

"We are going to go have dinner there, so we can get there early enough to get a good table near the dance floor. I haven't been to many on that side of town, but have heard that they get a good crowd over there."

"That sounds good to me. So are we all driving together?"

Margie Garrett

"Yes, I thought that we could all meet over at my place and we could go from here. Can you get here about seven?"

"Yes, I just need directions to get to your place."

"Good, well I will call you Saturday afternoon with the directions then."

"Okay, sounds good. I am curious to see how the parties are there."

"From what I remember, the bar isn't very big to hold the crowd; and they usually have a Disc Jockey and not a band. They are still pretty good though, just crowded."

"Do you know many singles actually go to those parties?"

"Not really."

"Okay, well thank you for inviting me to go with all of you. I have to go for now, so I will talk to you on Saturday then. Bye for now."

"Bye."

I was hoping that Donna would go to this party too, but she has to work Saturday, and it is kind of far for her she said. Well now that I know that I am going to go to this party. I am going to go online in the party forum and sign up for it.

While I was online, I took a few minutes to just check the messages. I have a couple just asking me how I am doing. None of the guys had asked me for a meet or to see if I was going to the party. In other words, none of the messages were worth answering right away about. I will answer them later.

Margie Garrett

With Crohn's Disease, I struggle every day of my life now. I never know where or when it will hit me. I am a strong woman and always have been. I mostly hide my feelings and pain from everyone, simply because people do not want to hear about all of the pain that I go through every day. This day has been pretty much a waste. I am going back to bed for the night. I had a very restless night. I didn't get much sleep at all, and I am still in a considerable amount of pain. As I wake up this morning, I absolutely refuse to be down again all day today beings that the party is tomorrow night. I have things to do today. I sure hope that I will feel better before tomorrow night's party. I am going to do my usual online check to see if there is anyone that I would be interested in meeting. I haven't talked to any of these guys, and I have no messages from any of the guys that are going to the party either. That is okay though. If nothing else, I am getting out of here for a little while. I am sure that I will have fun hanging out with my friends, and I can see how the host handles the party on this side of town.

It is already Saturday afternoon, and

I get a call from Janet, "Hi Margie, let me give you the directions to my place." And she did.

She then said, "If after the party, you don't want to drive all of the way home, you can stay here. Some of the other guys said they were going too.

"Okay, good. Thanks. Okay, well I still have to figure out what I am going to wear, so I will be there around seven o'clock then."

"Okay, see you then."

Well, it is time for me to leave already. So I am going to head over to Janet's now, and from there we had gone to the party. When we had arrived, there were not too many people there yet, so we were able to get a table by the dance floor. I told myself this time, that I was not just going to sit there all night. I was glad to see that Janet and the rest were not waiting for the guys to ask us to dance. We went out on the dance floor with or without the guys. We had a blast. As I look around, I see that most of the guys there at the party, were like wall flowers, not moving at all. They sure didn't look like they were having any fun at all. That was their choice though. It isn't like there weren't enough women. There is quite a crowd here. I still haven't been asked to dance, but that is okay with me.

All of us ended up staying over at Janet's tonight. It was very nice of her to let us, and then she made us all breakfast in the morning too. We stayed over a couple hours after breakfast, talking about the party last night and then we went home.

I had a good time last night. I had realized though, that unless I start becoming a little more social and not so afraid of talking to people, that I don't know that things are ever going to get any better for me. I have to learn to be more comfortable and be more of a people person.

One way of forcing myself to get past my shyness, is to host some parties myself. As a hostess, you are forced to talk to your guests. People you know and the people that you have never met before. So, the ultimate question is, do I really want to go that far, or do I want to continue doing it this way. I know that I probably will continue to stay in my shell if I don't change what I am doing. Hosting a party though, that is a very big commitment, and a lot of responsibility.

Over the next couple of weeks, I continued looking into what is involved in the process of hosting a singles party. I have to abide by all of the rules of the site in hosting a party. I can't have a party location close to another host on the same weekend. I can't accept any money from any of the guests. The cover charge for entry to the party has to be posted, along with many other rules. I need to find a good venue that can accommodate a large party, because there cannot be a minimum amount or a maximum amount of guests for any party. Then, when that is all done, I would need to choose the day that I would want to have one and post the party online for the guests to sign up for it. Amongst all of that, I would also want other things outside the normal site rules. Things that I decide for my parties that will make them my own and am similar to other hosts, but not exactly the same either. If I am going to do this, I want my guests to really enjoy themselves. I want everything to be perfect. I know that it won't be, at least not the first few parties. That is if I do anymore parties after the first one.

I called Donna, "Hi Donna, what are you doing?"

"Hi Margie, I am just hanging around here checking messages and chatting with Dan."

"Oh, so have you met him yet?"

"No, I haven't answered him yet. We have been talking for a few days now though."

"He hasn't asked you to meet him yet?"

"No, but I did notice that he is going to the next party, so I am going to this one. One way or another, I am going to get that night off of work."

"How is everything else going?"

"Good. How are you doing? Are things getting any better for you? I really do worry about you."

"I know that you do. I will be fine though. You really don't need to worry so much. I am starting to go out more often. I went to the last party too. So things are getting a little better"

"Good, I am glad to hear that. Oh, Dan is on is on the other line. I have to go, I will talk to you later."

"Okay, bye."

You know what, I am going to call Janet, and ask her what she thinks about me hosting a party and just see what she thinks about it. So I did call Janet,

"Hi Janet, how are you today?"

"Hi Margie, what's happening?"

"Not too much. I wanted to see what you think about me hosting a party."

"Wow, are you kidding. Do you really want to take that on?"

"Well, it might be good for me. It will force me to start talking to others, instead of just sitting there all of the time."

"That is a big responsibility, and an awful lot of planning that is involved in it."

"I know, and I am probably crazy, but I just think it will be good for me to do this."

"Well, did you know that our host, Brian, now has decided that he is tired of doing the parties, and that this next party is probably going to be last one that he will be hosting? I don't see any other party for the east side posted after this one. So, this would be a perfect time for you to do this. Hosting the parties is really hard though. You will be getting a lot of feedback, both good and bad."

"Well, hopefully, it will be mostly good. I am going to start the planning then, and get things started. I only have a couple of weeks to find the venue and everything, and then I need to post it too."

"Well, I sure wish you luck. If you need any help, just let me know okay."

"I will let you know, thanks. Well, I have to go. I will talk to you later."

"Okay, bye.

So, the planning begins. I go online and pull up a list of all of the clubs locally and see which ones have entertainment for the weekends. I look at their capacity, location, whether they have live bands or Disc Jockeys, cover charges, parking fees, whether they generally have a young, or an older crowd, or is it a mixture of both young and old on the weekends. How big the dance floor is and where it is located in the club. Is it in the front, back, or the center? How the tables are arranged and how many they have in the club, also, if the club serves food and how late they will serve food.

After checking some of the clubs online, I have narrowed it down to four of them. There are two clubs that are on the east side, and two on the west side. The names of the clubs that I have chosen are, Kitty Korner Bar, Do Drop Inn, Nowhere Bar, and Big Escape Bar and Grill. Now, I just need to call all of them tomorrow, and set up a time to meet with management to discuss my plans and ask them questions about what I would want from them. Right now, I need to sit down and make out a list of the questions that I want to ask them. I don't need to ask any of them about the capacity, because all of the clubs are large enough to accommodate a big crowd, nor do I have to ask about parking fee, because they all have free parking. They, also, all serve food, but I do need to find out how late they will serve. I need to ask them if the cover charge can be waived for all the members. Also, if I can reserve seating, and if so, how many tables that I can reserve for the night, and if I can do any decorations and what they will allow. I need to ask them what the earliest that I can get into the club before the parties to set up. Also need to ask, if I can get the drinks discounted for the members for like an hour or so throughout the night. I, also, need to ask, whether I can choose the band that plays for the party, and, if I can advertise their establishment on the site for the party.

Once, I meet with all four of the clubs and discuss all of this and their decisions on what the arrangements would be, then I will make my decision on which one I will host the party at. At least, I have narrowed the choices down to the four. Actually, I really only have to worry about the two on the east side, because the first party will be on this side of town. I already know that there is no other party for around here booked for three weeks from now. So I am thinking that I will do it, if everything goes okay with the club, on June twelfth. That will give me three weeks. And, hopefully, that date will work for the club too.

Well, I am exhausted, I think that I am going to put this down for a while and check my messages and just relax with a glass of wine for the rest of the night. I go online and I had several messages, mostly just guys saying hi and introducing themselves. You won't even believe this. One of the messages was from a kid that is my sons' age, he said that he hopes that I don't mind his age, but that he loves older woman. That they are much more mature, and that he could give me a night that I would never forget.

I couldn't believe the message. Are you kidding me? It is totally unbelievable some of the messages that I get. I am hardly going to go out with a kid my son's age. Are you kidding me? I don't think so. I messaged this kid back and told him that he needs to find a lady that is more his age and that I don't mean to be rude, but that age is definitely a factor, and that I am just not interested. I did say in the message though, that I wish him luck in finding her. I left it at that.

I was, actually, amazed at some of these messages. It is almost like some of these men are desperate. Why else would they be interested in the older woman, unless, of course, they are looking for a woman with a lot of money. Oh, here is another one, good grief, this one is in his twenties and I sent him the same message back. This one replies back and said to think of it this way. With him being younger that he can go a lot longer than guys my age. This is truly unbelievable. I thought to myself, ok, two can play this game, so I messaged him back and said to him, honey you wouldn't be able to keep up with me. I may be older, but I certainly am not dead.

As I sit here laughing and waiting for his reply back. He was laughing and said to me in the reply that it would be fun to try. I replied back that it would only be in his dreams. That it was a nice try though. Why is it that the only messages that I am getting, so far, are from the young kids, the old men like fifteen years older, or the sex maniacs that are just looking for a night of fun and sex, as they put it? I can't seem to get any decent guys contact me. Oh, if nothing else, it is entertaining. Well, I have had enough for the night. I really can't deal with anymore maniacs tonight. I am going to bed and hopefully can set up those appointments in the morning. Right now, I am so tired though. Off to bed I go. Sure hope that I can fall off to sleep. I am so anxious right now. I need to try though.

As I wake up this morning, I was still so tired; I was restless all night, which is exactly what I thought it would be. I just have so much on my mind these days. I am going to just put a pot of coffee on and call and make these appointments with the Nowhere Bar and Kitty Korner Bar. I sure hope that they will agree to what I want. Well, here I go.

I am calling the Nowhere Bar first. The phone is ringing and they answer, "Nowhere Bar, can I help you?"

"Hi, this is Margie; can I speak with the manager please?"

"Can I ask what you are calling about?"

"I am calling in regards to possibly holding a singles party with you. I am with an online dating site called BDE, which is Best Dating Ever. Is there a possibility of talking to someone about it?"

"Sure, hold on, I will get Tom for you. He would be the one that would handle all of that."

"Thanks that would be great."

Tom comes to the phone, "Hi Margie, this is Tom, how can I help you?"

Margie Garrett

"Hi Tom, I am looking into hosting a singles party in a couple of weeks. In looking at different clubs in the area, I had decided to give you a call. Your establishment is very nice, and in a good location. I just have some questions for you. Is there any way that we can, maybe, meet and discuss this?"

"Sure, I can't do it today, but how about five o'clock tomorrow? Do you think that would be good for you?"

"Yes, that would be great. I will see you tomorrow then."

"Okay Bye."

So, now that one is set up. Now I will call Kitty Korner Bar. Hopefully, I can get with them today. That would be great if I can.

I called them and asked, "Hi, this is Margie, could I speak to a manager in regards to hosting a singles party there?"

"Let me see if Jim is around. He is the one you would need to talk to."

"Okay, thanks."

"Hi Margie, this is Jim. I understand that you want to host a singles party here?"

"Yes, I wanted to know if maybe I could meet with you today, if you aren't too busy."

"Today is good. Can you wait until after the dinner rush though? Can you come about seven o'clock?"

"I sure can, thanks."

"Okay, well I sell see you then."

"Okay, I look forward to meeting you. Bye."

Margie Garrett

Wow, this is great. Kitty Korner Bar seems like it might be the one. I haven't even met Jim yet and I already get the impression that he might be very accommodating and easy to work with. I can't wait until tonight to meet with him. I didn't even think of today being a Saturday. I will, actually, get to see the entertainment if I stay long enough too.

I still can't believe that I am even considering doing this. I am starting to get nervous now though. Doing this is not an easy task for me. Kind of a very big step in the right direction though. I need to show myself that I can do anything I set my mind to do. This is going so fast, and I was definitely not prepared.

I need to dress up, somewhat professional looking. I sure can't go in my blue jeans. I have to find something to wear and quickly. I know what I can wear, that black skirt and top that I wore when Jon took my photos. I look good in it. What is nice for me too, is that Kitty Korner Bar is only a couple of miles from my house. I don't have far to drive either.

Well, it is about five o'clock; it is time to start getting ready here. I need a pen and all of the questions that I wrote down to ask Jim. I am sitting here asking myself, "What in the world am I doing? Am I crazy?" I still can't believe that I am going through with this and am actually going to be a hostess of a big singles party. I am though.

It is now time for me to shower and change into my clothes. As I am getting ready to walk out of the door, I think, to make sure that I haven't forgotten anything, and that I have no other questions that I need to ask Jim. Everything is good to go.

I arrive a few minutes early. I take a deep breath and reassure myself, before I get out of my jeep, that I can do this. I walk inside and go up to bar, and I let them know that I have an appointment with Jim.

The bartender said, "I will go get Jim for you. Margie would you like a drink on the house?"

"Thank you, can I have a draft beer, anything is good?"

"Sure, if you want to sit at one of the tables, I will get you that beer and if you can give Jim just a couple of minutes. He is finishing up some paperwork."

"Okay, no problem. I am just thankful that he could meet with me tonight."

"Actually, when he told me why you were meeting him, he is pretty excited about the thought of holding a party like that."

"He will be over here in a few minutes. I have to get back to work."

"Okay, thanks."

After a couple of minutes, Jim comes over to my table with his book and says,

"Hi Margie"

"Hi Jim, I want to thank you for meeting me tonight. I have to be honest, I have never been here. You have a very nice establishment here and your staff is really friendly. I like that."

"Well, thank you."

"You are very welcome."

"I hear that you want to hold a singles party here?"

"Yes, actually I would."

"So what is this dating site and tell me what you would need or want from me."

"Well, I represent an online dating site called BDE which stands for Best Dating Ever. The parties that have been hosted in the area, range anywhere from fifty to three hundred members. What I am looking for is a venue that can accommodate a crowd like that, which obviously, you can here. I would like to be able to be a part of the decision for the band playing the night of the party. The parties would always be on a Saturday night. Is that possible to do with you?"

"Yes, Saturday nights are fine. I have the bands booked months in advance though. So you would have to book your party on the weekend of when that band is performing though."

"That is fine, I can do that. I also wanted to know if you would waive the cover charge for the members."

"Absolutely, if you pull in a crowd like that, I sure will waive all cover charges for the members. They will just need to let the bouncer at the door know that they are with BDE and there will be no problem there."

"Can I also get reserved seating preferably close to the dance floor?"

"I can give you reserved seating, but I need to keep some for my regulars."

"I totally understand. How much seating can I reserve? Can I get them close to the dance floor?"

"I will give you all of these tables from the dance floor to half way back. That gives you about twenty tables. What do you think; will that be good for you?"

"Perfect. Now, I think the only other thing is decorations. Can I decorate before the parties, and do you have any restriction, also, how early can I do it before the parties?"

"The only thing that I ask is that there is no confetti and you can come in a couple of hours before the party to do any decorations."

"I am going to have a sign in book; do you have a stand or something to put at the front door, so they can sign in when they arrive?"

"We can find something, I am sure. Do you know when you were thinking about holding the first party?"

"I am thinking about June twelfth. Would that be okay with you? I don't know how many will show on a first party. Once they are regular parties here, if you allow me to hold them here, the parties will grow for sure."

"Well, June twelfth is fine, and actually if you would like to stay, the band performing tonight will be the band for your party. I am sure that you will like them."

"Cool, I will stay for a while then. So, can I assume that you agree to me holding the parties here and the date then?"

"Yes, I am actually looking forward to seeing how this works out for both of us."

"I am too. To be honest with you, this will be my first one."

"Well, looks to me, like you are going to put on a great party."

"Oh, there is one more thing. I don't know if you would do something like a Happy Hour in the middle of the night, where they can get discounted drinks."

"I can do better than that; the beers will be two dollars all night. How is that?"

"Wow that would be great. Thank you so much."

"No, thank you. I am sure that my business will pick up with the parties."

"Well, I think this will be good for both of us. Can I get you another beer?"

"Yes, thanks." "Be right back."

I couldn't believe this. For some reason, I am thinking the Nowhere Bar isn't going to come close to being the cooperative. I will meet with them though out of respect and maybe for a backup venue, but I am sure that this is where I want my parties to be.

Jim comes back with my beer and said to me, "Well, Margie, I look forward to working with you on your parties. I have to get back to work. The band will be starting soon. I have instructed my staff to get you anything that you would like to eat or drink on the house tonight."

"Wow, you don't have to do that."

"I know, but I want to. Stay and enjoy yourself."

"I will and thank you. I will give you a call next week."

"That sounds good."

I am pretty proud of myself right now. I handled myself very well with Jim. However, now here I sit at a table in a bar all by myself. All of the sudden, the insecurities are back. I don't know how long I will stay. I want to stay long enough to see how the band is though. Luckily, I wasn't bothered by anyone. After a while of listening, I had gone up to the bar and told them to have a good night and to thank Jim for me. Then I had left.

I went straight home and then straight to bed thoroughly exhausted. As soon as my head hit the pillow and I was down I fell asleep. I slept very hard and all through the night without waking at all.

When I woke up the next morning, I had decided to go online to see how the other hosts post the parties, and what is put on there to do the advertisement for them. I needed to figure out how to do all of this. Janet sure was right, when she told me that it would be a lot of work. I didn't realize, I guess how much is actually involved in the planning and hosting of a party, until I started looking into it.

Today, I am going to the Nowhere Bar to meet with Tom. In asking Tom the exact same questions, he told me that he would waive the cover charge for all of the members that would be arriving before nine o'clock, but that any of them that would be coming in any later would have to pay. Tom also said that he wouldn't be able to reserve as many table as I would have wanted. He also said that he wouldn't be able to discount any of the drinks for an hour if the cover charge is waived.

The atmosphere in the Nowhere Bar was not as nice either. In other words, the whole idea of a party here is going nowhere. Sorry for the pun. This place just isn't working for me. Tom is not as friendly as Jim either. It is just not really a place that I would ever want to hold the parties at. I didn't even get past the first couple of questions here. That was really all that I needed to make my decision.

To be honest, I couldn't get out of there fast enough. Tom asked me when I would be holding my party. I just told him that I wasn't sure yet, and that I would give him a call when I had made my decision. We shook hands and I said good night and then I left.

Now, after only two days of deciding I was going to this. I already have the venue and the date all set up. Tomorrow I need to post the party on the site. I need to put together all of the information that will be posted.

As I wake up this morning, sitting here with my coffee, I am feeling pretty good about what I have done over the last couple of days. Seems, that the activities of deciding and planning these parties has somehow taken away from me all of the feelings of depression and hopelessness that I have had in the past. I am feeling a little bit better about myself in accomplishing this. I think that I am just going to take some time to take this all in and relax and enjoy my coffee this morning. It actually just feels good to take a little time to breathe and absorb everything that I have been able to accomplish in such a short time. I really want to put together a great party that everyone will want to come to again and again.

To be a hostess, as I said before, is something that I have never really thought about doing. This, if nothing else, I will be able to recover my self-confidence and my self-esteem that I once had.

Margie Garrett

Right now, I don't have the time to think about my past issues and how lonely I am. Doing this party is helping me keep focused on moving forward in my life, and not looking at how hurt that I was in my past all of the time, which is exactly what I need.

As I prepare what I think that I will be putting in the post for the party, I think I need to put a catchy phrase to open the invitational post. I am not sure about that yet. I will figure it out though, I can always put that up later if I figure something out, in the meantime, I will just put the name of the bar, Kitty Korner, and the date of June twelfth at nine o'clock for a night of mixing and mingling and a whole lot of dancing. You won't regret it; you will all have a great time. Then I will finish the post with the address and the directions with the sign up below, and of course, put myself at the top as the hostess for the night. There it is, all posted on the site now.

Now I will just see what happens. I sure am curious to see how many of the members will actually sign up for the party. I, now, just wait and watch and also monitor my post and all of the replies and comments that are posted in the forum for the upcoming party. I am so excited about this.

I am going to call Jim at Kitty Korner now,

"Hi, this is Margie, is Jim there, by any chance?"

"Yes he is, let me go get him for you."

"Okay, thanks."

Jim comes on the phone and he says, "Hi Margie, how are things going with the party?"

"They are going very well. I thought that I would call you and let you know that I have now posted the party and that the members will now be able to sign up. I will be able to give you updates on how many will be coming from week to week now."

"Cool, I am so glad that you have decided to hold your parties here."

"Well, just remember please, that I don't know exactly how many will come to this first one. I am sure that the parties will get bigger as I do more of them."

"Well, any business you can bring in here will help. So, again thank you."

Margie Garrett

"You are welcome. Well, I am going to go home for now, I will call you next week with an update."

"Okay, thank you, you have a great night."

"I hope that you do too. Bye."

Well, the work for now is done. I went offline for a while and went for a walk to get out of the house. I really needed a break from everything. I went out to clear my head. It actually feels good to put my mind at rest at least for a little while. It seems like my mind has been racing for the last few days.

Wow, I am actually a hostess now. I have so many emotions. I am excited, nervous, and actually terrified. Will I be able to be to be able to be a good hostess that everyone deserves? Can I really pull this off, with as shy as I am, faking it the whole night, mixing and mingling with everyone. I am definitely going to try very hard to make these parties fun for everyone.

This isn't just a big step, but a huge step out of my comfort zone. I am doing it though. I still can't believe that I am actually doing this.

It is now a couple of hours since I had posted the party online. I wonder if I should check the post yet to see if anyone has signed up. I had decided that I would wait until later to find out if anyone has signed up.

My phone is ringing and it is Janet. "Hi Margie, you have been a very busy lady, haven't you?"

"What do you mean?"

"I saw the post for the party, and of course, I had signed up for the party. I wouldn't miss it. I can't believe that you put it together so fast. Good Job!"

"Thanks Janet. I figured, why wait, if I am going to do it, then I better get moving with it."

"Well, you sure didn't waste any time."

"Do you think that many people will come?"

"I don't know, but I am sure you will have a good crowd. It might be small this time, but who knows about the next one. I am sure that it will depend on the feedback that people get from the first party."

"True, I am scared to death though. I sure hope that I can pull this off, and that everyone has a great time."

"I am sure that everyone will. You can do this, I am sure of it."

"I sure hope so."

"Well if there is anything that I can do to help you out, please let me know."

"I will Janet, thanks."

"Well, I have to get up early and I have another long day tomorrow, so I think that I am going to try and get some sleep. I will check in with you tomorrow and see how things are going"

"Okay, sleep well. Bye for now."

I know now, at the very least, I have one signed up now. Now I am really excited, because I didn't even tell Janet that I had posted the party. She had found out by looking for the local parties. Therefore, I know that others have seen the party post too. I can't help myself, I have to check and see what is happening on my party forum. How many have commented. Better than that, how many have actually signed up. I just have to see. I went online, after hanging up with Janet, and went to check it out. Wow, after only a few hours, I already have ten people signed up. And I have three weeks before the party. This is a great start for sure. I went on and commented thanking all that had signed up and said that I am looking forward to seeing them at Kitty Korner.

Now it is going to be very hard for me to not be checking it all of the time, now that all of the arrangements have been made, and the posting of the party is done. I am still not finished though. Now I need to decide on the decorations and check with Jim on a couple of other things. I am thinking too, that I need to get every member something to wear, so that the members can identify themselves from the normal crowd that goes there. I really don't want the normal name tags that a lot of the hosts give out, I really can't stand them.

I think that I am going to go to the party decorating store to see what I can find for that, as well as some of the decorations. That will be my next step. There is a pretty big store out by the mall that should have some of the things that I need. I know that it is open for a couple more hours tonight, so I know that I still have time to get there and check it out. I have to pay for all of this, so I don't want to spend too much money, and I need to find some of the things in bulk or at least pretty inexpensive, especially if I am going to have to get them for everyone and for every party that I may host. After this party, I will check online and see what I can find. This party though, I just don't have enough time to order anything, and I have to get it here in time for the party.

I think that I am going to head out there now, to see what they have. I had found some light wrist bracelets in two different colors, which would be good. They were red and blue, which are not that expensive if I buy a box of them. They come in a box of fifty. With this being my first party, I am really not expecting to have more than a hundred anyways. I am going to get a box of each.

As far as the decorations for the party, I think that I am just going to buy about six sets of three helium balloons that have BDE on them representing the dating site, and put them around the table where the reserved seating will be. That should decorate the place up for the party. I do have to check with Jim though, to see if I can do this, but I am also thinking about putting out a couple of little bowls on the tables and have some snacks in them for the people to munch on, while they are drinking.

That will depend on how many people actually sign up for the party, and how much money that I have left in the planning for this party. I may, also, order some appetizers from the kitchen too. Again, I won't make that decision, until I actually see how many people show up. I will decide that the night of the party as to whether or not I am going to do that.

Well, it looks like everything is in place for an unbelievable party. Now that all of the planning is done, arrangements have all been made, and the party has been posted with the sign up already, all I need to do now is answer all of the replies both in my inbox, and in the party forum. Also I am now just monitoring the forum thread to make sure that all members stay within the party forum guidelines.

I am so tired tonight. I have had, yet once again, a very busy day. I can't help, but to go online and check to see how many members have signed up for the party before I go to get some rest for the night, and so I did just that. There are only a couple more members that have signed up so far, but this is only the second day that it has been posted. There is almost three weeks before the party, and there is plenty of time yet. Most people won't commit to going to the party until sometimes only a couple of days before the actual party date. I am certainly not worried yet about how many will actually be coming. I am going to go to bed now, both sore and totally exhausted.

I keep asking myself if I can really go through with this party. It is one thing to plan a party like this, but to be a really good hostess who has absolutely no problem with being very sociable with total strangers is certainly not going to be easy for me to do. I really have no choice, I am just going to have to now, with all of the preparations and date and party posted with me as the hostess. I have a couple of weeks now to prepare myself. Maybe, just talking to some of the members online will help with my uneasiness of hosting this party. I sure hope so.

As a hostess, I need to look like one too. I can't exactly go and host a party like this dressed in blue jeans. I am going to have to find something really nice to wear, and since I am single, something that will make me look really hot would be nice too. What am I going to wear? I am really going to have to think about this one.

Wow, Donna is calling me; I haven't talked with her in a very long time.

"Hi Donna, how have you been?"

"I am good. It looks like you have been on very busy lady lately."

"Yes, this party is keeping me very busy."

"I think that is great. It is taking your mind off of all the past, which is exactly what you needed to do."

"It sure is helping me. Actually, I am pretty excited about hosting this party. I just hope that everyone has a really good time."

"Have you had any dates lately?"

"No, I will only meet the men at the parties now."

"What if they don't go to the parties, then what?"

"Well, they won't meet me, because this is the only way I will meet any men now. It just has to be this way for now."

"I totally understand."

"How are the plans going for the party? Do you need any help with anything?"

"To be honest, I am all set. I have already made all of the arrangements. I have all of the decorations and everything that I need. Now, I am just checking the site every day, and answer all of the comments. Most importantly though, I have been checking to see how many have signed up for the party, which is what I was getting ready to do when you called."

"I just went to sign up for the party and there are twenty eight people so far."

"Are you kidding me?"

"No, that is what the count was about an hour ago."

"I can't believe that there is already that many. There is still two more weeks to sign up."

"Well, that is a good thing. It is looking like you are going to have a great crowd for the part."

"It sure is looking good so far."

"So how have you been feeling? How has your Crohns Disease been, any better lately?"

"No, it is about the same. There is really no change. I have learned to live with all of the pain though. What else can I do?"

"Nothing, I guess. I just do not like seeing you in so much pain all of the time."

"No big deal, I will be fine. Doing this party is taking my mind off of it for the most part. I haven't been to bad lately. I have my good days and my bad. I cope with it though."

"Well, I am glad that you are doing fine for now then."

"Yes, me too, I am pretty tired tonight though."

"Well go get some rest and we can talk again tomorrow."

"Yes, I think that I am going to go to bed. I will text you in the morning. Okay?"

"Good night."

"See you for now."

I went to bed totally exhausted again. When I woke up the next morning, I was not feeling good at all. I guess that I should not have opened my big mouth telling Donna how good I had been feeling. Obviously, I will not be doing anything or going anywhere today. I am all cramped up and in serious pain this morning. Guess I will make a pot of coffee this morning and just try and relax, which is really not that easy when I am feeling like this. Sometimes drinking something hot will help with the pain though. I sure hope that it does.

Today is definitely going to be a lazy day for me. I just can't do a whole lot when I am feeling like this. I am mostly in the bed when I am feeling like this. I didn't even feel like going on to the computer and check the site. I have just no ambition to do anything but lay around. The coffee is not working this morning at all.

I went back to the bed all curled up in pain and tears. I hate feeling like this, so helpless and hopeless. Right now, I sure wish that I had a man who loves me and would be here to comfort me through this, but I don't. The horrible thing is that I am afraid that I will never have a man in my life that will love me like that. Let's face it, most people don't want to get involved and attached to someone with any illness. They want a healthy partner, and I really can't fault them for feeling that way, not at all. There is no harm in dreaming about having that special man in my life though. We all have dreams.

As I lay here, crying from all of the pain, I decided to take a pain pill. I don't like taking them because they just knock me out. When the pain is this severe, I really don't have much of a choice unless I want to continue hurting this badly. I did take the pill as much as I didn't want too. It is now four o'clock in the afternoon, and I haven't been back out of the bed since I had gone to lay back down this morning. I just can't seem to move today at all. About an hour or so after taking the pain pill, I finally did fall off to sleep. When I finally did wake up it was hours later; and am very tired now and feeling so weak and dizzy. Which is exactly what that pill will do to me? As much as I don't like taking the pill; it sure does help relieve some of the pain.

As long as I am up for a while, I better go check the site and make sure that everything is fine and to check the count for the upcoming party. When I went online, I was just totally amazed that I already have over thirty people signed up. I also went to check my inbox for any new mail. Much to my surprise, I am being bombarded with new messages from both men and woman. Most of the messages were either to thank me for hosting the party, or they had some questions about it.

Either way, I am not up for answering any of them. I just can't do it tonight. After I had checked out the site, I just went back to bed. I just can't seem to keep my eyes open. I didn't wake back up until the next morning.

Well, it is another day; and I am actually feeling a little bit better this morning. I, now, need to answer all of those messages from last night that I didn't answer. This ought to take me most of the day since there are so many of them. I knew there was a lot of work to do with all of the party planning. What I didn't realize or think about would be all of the messages and questions that I would have to deal with on top of that. This really is a lot of work. I am, so far, having fun though.

It is now one week before the party. Now, I am really starting to get nervous. I have to make any last minute arrangements and am now really watching the sign up list. After not checking for almost a day, yesterday, I went online to take care of some things. Much to my surprise, the sign up list has now grown to over fifty members and it is still growing.

I called Jim at Kitty Korner to give him the update.

"Hi Jim, this is Margie."

"Hi Margie, how is everything going for the party?"

"Well, that is why I am calling. I thought that I would let you know the latest head count now for the party. I have over fifty members signed up so far."

"Wow that is great. I am really looking forward to this party and seeing how many members will actually come. I just hope everything goes well for all of you. I will try my best."

"Well, I think the both of us will. This party will be my first for hosting."

"From what I see, you are going to have a great party and be an awesome hostess. If there is anything else you need please just let me know."

"I will Jim, thank you. Well I better get back to work. I will call you on Friday with the last update before the party."

"Okay, I will talk with you later. Bye."

"Bye Jim."

I continue checking and answering all of my messages, I get a message from a man who doesn't live to far from me. His name is Bob. He pretty much just introduced himself, and said that I was pretty and that he likes what I say in my profile. I responded back laughingly and said that he needs to get his eyes checked. Pretty, I don't think so. He answered back that there is absolutely nothing wrong with his eyes. I thanked him for the compliment though.

What a long day this has been for me. I, to be honest, didn't think it would ever end for me. I have only a week now to prepare myself for what is going to be a very difficult night for me. Not only do I have to be a very outgoing and confident person, which I am not, one that can just have a conversation with anyone. Which, I am not that that way at all. I sure hope that I can do this, and that everyone has a really good time. I am going to try real hard to make this party the best ever.

Over the next few days, I try to work on myself and my image that I have to portray. I start talking to people on the site that are signed up for the party. That way, I will have at least talked with some of them. I still have to figure out what to wear to the party.

Oh, Janet is calling me; maybe she can help me figure out what to wear.

"Hi Janet, how are you?"

"I am great; I am really looking forward to the party tomorrow night."

"I am so nervous. I keep thinking that there is something I am missing. I guess that I am not though. I have no idea what to wear to the party yet though. Do you have any suggestions"

"Yes, actually, do you remember the black one piece pantsuit that was low in the front and had the open back? The one you had on for that first party that we had gone too. You looked great that night. Are you going to get your hair and nails done tomorrow?"

"Oh my, I didn't even think about that one."

"Well if you want, I can come over tomorrow and help you get ready."

"I have to be at Kitty Korner around seven o'clock to do all of the decorations too."

"Well, that is okay. Well I can help you with them, and we can have some dinner, and try and relax the rest of the night."

"I don't know about relaxing, this is going to be so hard for me to act like a totally different and confident person."

"You will be fine. We are all going to have a great time. You will see."

"I sure hope so, but any help that you can give me will be so appreciated. That is for sure."

"Okay, well I will be over your house around noon tomorrow then."

"Thanks Janet, I will see you then. Bye."

"Bye."

It is now about nine o'clock Friday night. I went online to check the party, and I now have seventy three members that will be attending the party. This is great. I never really expected this many people would attend. I called Jim, as I promised him that I would, to give him the final update. I am going to try and get a good night sleep tonight. I really need it.

Before going to bed, I received an instant message from Bob. Apparently Bob didn't know anything about me hosting a singles party tomorrow night. He asked me

"What are you up to these days?"

Margie Garrett

I answered "I am just preparing for the party tomorrow night."

"Can I possibly meet you earlier in the day then?"

I regretfully told him "I am very sorry but I can't meet you earlier in the day. Is there a possibility that you could come to the party, we could meet there for a drink and some dancing"

He said "I am really not into going to the bars, it just isn't my scene."

"Unfortunately, that is really the only way that I am meeting any men now, I have had just way to many bad experiences outside the parties lately."

"Well I would really prefer not to go to the parties."

It is quite obvious that I am probably not going to hear from Bob again, which is a real shame because he seems like a really nice man, one that I would love to meet. I just can't outside of the parties though, I just can't.

Well, I am off to bed now. I have a very long and extremely stressful day ahead of me. The anxiety is really setting in now for me. I lay here for a couple of hours, unable to clear my head enough to fall asleep. My brain seems to be racing with all kinds of thoughts and emotions. I can't seem to relax enough tonight. This doesn't surprise me at all though. I am so excited and extremely nervous about hosting this party at the same time. I might as well just get out of bed, put a pot of coffee on and start my day.

I went back online and I posted a comment on my party and said thank you for all that have decided to come tonight. And that I hope that they all have a great time, and that I look forward to meeting each and every one of them tonight. The count now stands at seventy five, which is more than what I had ever anticipated for a first party.

It is now about ten o'clock in the morning. Janet will be over in a couple of hours to help me get ready. I am going to go take a shower and wash my hair. I have some white nail polish; so I am going to give myself a French manicure and pedicure before Janet gets here. I have to find all of my jewelry too and put on my make-up. I need to look really hot tonight, which sure isn't very easy for me either. I sure hope that the pantsuit looks as good on me this time as it did before.

Cool Janet is here.

"I am so glad that you are here, I am a nervous wreck."

"You are going to be just fine."

"I am so glad that you have such confidence in me, because I sure don't know how I am going to pull this off."

"Trust me, you are going to look great and you will be awesome tonight. You can do this."

"Thanks."

"Well, let's get your hair curled and put up."

"Okay."

Janet has my hair all done now.

"Wow, Janet thanks, I really like it."

"Now, go get your pantsuit on and let's see how you look."

"I found my black necklace and earrings to go with the pantsuit too."

"Great."

And so I go get dressed, put on my jewelry, and Janet touched up my facial make-up a little bit.

And she said to me

"You look great Margie. Just like a perfect singles party hostess, both hot and sexy."

"Well, I sure wouldn't go that far, but thank you for the compliment."

"What time do we need to be there?"

"I figure that I should be there around seven o'clock to make sure that everything is ready"

"We have about an hour or so then before we need to go. Do you want me to see if the party count has changed at all since last night?"

"Yes, if you would."

"Okay then, I am going to go check for you. Wow, Margie, you now have eighty seven coming to the party."

"I am so nervous Janet."

"You will be just fine."

"Please, keep telling me that. I still can't believe that I am even doing this."

"I can't believe that you managed to put this all together as quickly as you did."

"I can't believe I did either, but once I set my mind to do something, I don't stop."

"I can sure see that."

"Do I look okay?"

"Yes you do."

"Well, I guess that we better get going, so that I can do all of the finishing touches then."

"Okay, let's do it."

We arrive at Kitty Korner, I have to make sure that all of the tables are reserved, that there are reserved signs on all of them, and that the head tables says hostess table on it. Then I need to put all of the balloons around the area to decorate the area, and put out all of the bowls of snack at every table.

Jim had come in and said to me,

"Wow, Margie, it really looks great in here. Can I get you anything?"

"Hi Jim, this is Janet, by the way."

"Hi Janet, It is nice to meet you."

"It is nice to meet you too Jim."

I said to Jim,

"I think that we are all set here, I think that we are going to get a bite to eat before everyone starts coming in."

"Well, anything that you two want, I will take care of your tab for the night Margie."

"Thank you so much Jim."

"Just let me know what you would like when you are ready."

"Actually, I think that we want an order of chicken strips and I would like a bud light. What about you Janet?"

Janet said,

"I would like a diet Pepsi, thank you."

"Okay, I will get that for you two."

"Thanks Jim."

Janet had said to me,

"Margie, just relax, you look great, and the place looks great. Everything will be fine. Just say hello to everyone when they walk in. Walk around and mix and mingle and you will be fine. Breathe."

"I am trying to. Oh my God, people are starting to come in already."

Margie Garrett

"Just go say hi and introduce yourself."

"Okay, here I go."

And so, as nervous as I am, I went over to them and said,

"Hi, are you with BDE?"

"Yes we are."

"Hi, I am Margie, your hostess, how are all of you tonight?"

"Hi, I am John; this is Brian, Larry, and Ed."

"I have a reserved table that I have saved that will seat quite a few members, if you would like too you can sit there. It is close to the dance floor too."

"That would be great. There are more of our friends coming. We still have Debbie, Michelle and Kelly coming too. Is there going to be enough room at your table for three more?"

"Yes, you can all sit there. There is more than enough room. I will be right back; I need to take care of something."

Take care of something for sure, like catch my breath. I am just a total wreck.
I had gone back to the table and said thanks to Janet for helping me with everything.

It is now nine o'clock, and the place is pretty full. The band will be starting in about a half an hour. Jim came over to my table with a jigger of Washington Apple and several shot glasses. I gave everyone at my table and shot, and I thanked Jim.

Well, now that everyone is here, or at least most everyone; I need to start really mixing and mingling with everyone and become a good hostess with a smile on my face, and making sure that everyone is having a good time.

I didn't have a whole lot of time to sit down at my table, because I am so busy making sure that everything is going well. I took my camera out and started taking some pictures of everyone, on the dance floor and off of it.

Jim came up to me and said,

"Margie, you put together a great party; everyone looks like they are enjoying themselves."

"Yes, it sure looks like they are."

"Well, the dance floor is full and that is always a good sign."

"I am just so glad they all seem to be enjoying themselves."

"Good job."

"Thanks Jim."

"No, I need to thank you Margie, for putting this party all together."

I went back to my table to sit down for a few minutes.

Janet said to me,

"Okay Margie, it is time for you to have some fun and enjoy yourself now. Let's go dance everyone." And so we all went out to the dance floor and had some fun.

I can now breathe a sigh of relief. From what I can tell, everyone is having a good time. I actually did it. I managed to pull it off, and I am pretty proud of myself, because I had absolutely no idea what I was doing or what I was getting myself into.

I am really glad that the night went well. It will be interesting to see the feedback from the people that came and what their thoughts were on the party. I can take the criticisms and use them to make the next one party even better. Wait a minute; I never said that I was going to do anymore parties. Based on all of the comments though, it looks like they are hoping that I will host more parties though. Most all of the comments were good. Personally, I had hoped to see more introductions between the members. I will need to figure out what I can do at the next party to make that happen.

The party was a lot of fun. I don't think that I did too badly, and I have decided that I will be doing more at Kitty Korner. Jim is very accommodating and good to work with. I am thinking that I will possibly hold another party on July third. I am not even going to plan this one yet. I have about a week that I can take and just relax and recoup. These parties really are more work than I had anticipated. I really enjoyed all of the planning, arrangements and being the hostess.

Everyone has been asking me when the pictures of the party will be uploaded on the site. I need to get to that this morning. I have never done this, so I am hoping that I can figure out how to do this. If not, I am sure that I can get Janet or someone to help me do it.

I have so many things to still do with the party. Between monitoring the site, replying to all of the comments, uploading all of the pictures and answering all of the messages in my inbox, it just seems like it is really never done. You have all of the work in planning, then the decorating, then the actual hosting of the party, and then all of the work afterwards. For a one night party, I actually have worked about three weeks minimum.

My phone is ringing, it is Janet calling me.

"Hi Janet."

"Hi Margie, how are you feeling this morning? You have got to be pretty tired. I don't think that you stopped at all last night."

"No, I didn't stop; I am totally exhausted this morning."

"Yes, I bet that you are. Well you have time to relax now. By the way, you did a great job yesterday. I just thought I would let you know that. I know how worried you were and scared about talking to everyone, but like I said, you did a great job."

"Thanks Janet, I appreciate your saying that."

"You are very welcome. Do you think that you will be hosting another party?"

"Oh, I will for sure. I am thinking about have another party on July third with all of the Fourth of July decorations. I know that a lot of people will be gone for the holiday, but hopefully I can have enough of a turn out that it will be a nice smaller party. I won't have to work quite as hard either. I am still deciding though."

"You are right; there will be a lot of people that will be out of town, so you won't have to work quite as hard as you did with this one."

"All that I know is that I am going to take the next few days and relax. I will let Kitty Korner know that I will be doing another party that night, but that is all that I am doing for right now."

"I don't blame you, you definitely deserve a break."

"Well, I better get back to getting all of these pictures from last night uploaded. A lot of people are asking to see them, so I will talk to you later."

"Okay, see you for now. Bye."

"Bye."

I didn't realize how many pictures that I had taken last night. This is going to take me a while to upload all of them. It took me at the very least a couple of hours, but they are all uploaded and now on the site for everyone to see, and finally the works done. Now I am going to go lay down for a little while. I am so exhausted.

When I woke up, I had gone back online to check any messages that I have. I have a few, but none that were of any importance. A couple of them, I won't even answer back. They were from some men that just have one thing in mind. I guess their brain must be between their legs and they either don't know how to read or just didn't read my profile, either way, I found the messages very offensive and so I just deleted and blocked them from ever contacting me again, unbelievable.

Oh great, now I get an instant message. Who is this now? I am so not in the mood for conversations with anyone right now.

The window opens up with

"Hi beautiful."

I answered,

"Hi."

Margie Garrett

"What are you up to tonight?"

"Nothing, I am just relaxing. What about you?"

"Right now I am talking to you and looking at your pictures. Is that really you? You are gorgeous."

"Yes, those are my pictures. I am by far gorgeous, but thank you for the compliment."

"What are you doing on this site?"

"Same thing that you are, I hope anyways."

"And what is that?"

"I am looking for a guy in my life that will treat me right and respect me. What are you on here for?"

"I am on here to have some fun, of course, would you like to have some fun tonight?"

"Not really, I do wish you luck in finding someone tonight. I am just not into one night stands."

And so he closed his window out and went looking for someone else.

Why do I continue to attract the wrong men? I just don't get it. Why? I know that there has to be some good men out here. Where in the world are they hiding? I sure wish that I could find one that would restore my faith in the male gender.

Here I go again, another message.

This one says to me

"How would you like this body pressed up against you, caressing you, kissing you all over and making passionate love all through the night and into tomorrow. I can give you a night that you will for sure never forget. Think about it baby, and get back with me. I am sure that you will. How could you turn away this very muscular and toned body of mine? I am waiting for your reply."

Whatever, if he thinks I am going to respond, he will be waiting for a very long time. What a conceited moron. Are there that many desperate women that these guys send these kinds of messages to? Well, I am not one of them.

I, actually, have two good messages at least. Both messages were telling me what a great job that I did on hosting the party and that they had a blast and hope that I will be hosting more. I responded back to both of them thanking them and saying that I am glad that they had a good time and that I will be hosting more parties. I guess that I have to take the good messages with the bad ones. It just seems that the bad ones always seem to outnumber the good ones. I deal with it though, what else can I do? Actually, I am really surprised to say that there weren't many criticisms on the party like I had thought that there would be. This was a good sign for me.

I do want my parties different from the others, so that more people will want to come to mine. I need to come up with some ideas and things to do at mine that the other parties don't do. Maybe tomorrow, I will check on the internet for party suggestions and figure out if there are any suggestions that I can use in the club. No, I am not going to do it tomorrow, I said that I was going to take a couple of days off and just relax, and that is exactly what I am going to do.

Maybe this weekend I will just go out dancing and enjoy myself. That sounds like a plan. The question is where and who will I go out with. Especially, since I said that I wouldn't meet any men outside of the parties now. Can I trust any of them? I just don't know that I can. The last thing I want to do is to put myself in another dangerous date. I can't and won't do that.

I use to be pretty good at judging people, but not anymore. My judgment has failed me over and over again. If I never take chances though, I may never find the right man for me. I have put a big wall up around me now, and it is going to take one hell of a man, with an awful lot of patience and love, to break down that wall.

Maybe, I will go see Jon Gen perform this weekend if he is performing locally. I contacted him; unfortunately, he is performing in Ohio this weekend. I have no idea what to do now. I will probably end up just staying home alone.

Margie Garrett

I am getting so tired of being alone and lonely all of the time. I have to pull myself out of this major depression that I find myself in. I just don't know how to, or what I can do to get past all of these feelings of hopelessness. What can I do? No one can help me. I have to help myself; and I know that.

It is still very early in the week. Hopefully, I can figure out something to do this weekend, because I really don't want to sit around here alone. Maybe all of us girls can get together for a girls night out provided they don't all have plans already. It would be my luck that they do though.

Well, it is the end of the week; and it looks like I will be staying home, they all have dates or other plans for this weekend. It is probably just as well, because I don't feel very well anyways. I ended up spending most of the weekend in the bed sick and in a lot of pain.

Sometimes, I sit and wonder, if I will ever find a man that can be compassionate and loving enough to deal with me and all of my illnesses. Let's face it, most people will run at the sign of any medical issues. And I certainly have my ups and downs lately. Never really knowing from one day to the next how I will feel. Some days are definitely better than others; and sometimes there is just no way of hiding the pain.

It is now time to get the next party posted and set up. I call Jim and let him know and he said that he is looking forward to it. I made him aware of the fact that chances are that the party will be much smaller because of the holiday. He said that it wouldn't be a problem and that everything will still be the same as the last one. I thanked him and told him that I enjoy working with him on the parties.

A few days before the party, the count was at thirty one members, which was pretty good. That is almost half of what the last one was and this one is during the holiday which surprised me. I, to be honest, didn't think that I would have more than twenty sign up this time.

I think that I am only going to get two sets of six balloons in red, white and blue. I think that will be enough for decorating this time, besides; I really don't have much money to put out for this party. As I had said before, this party will be much smaller. I won't be working with it as much either. Just taking a few pictures, say hi to everyone and then I am actually going to relax and enjoy the night.

It is now the day before the party. I now have forty three coming. This is definitely a bigger party than I thought that it would be. Jim is amazed and thankful. He said that he was expecting a slow weekend for business; so he was surprised to hear how many are coming out for the party.

I really kind of hoped that I wouldn't have to dress up; but it is looking like I better whether I want to or not. What in the world am I going to wear? Maybe, I will wear my short black skirt and my brown low cut top that is gathered at the waist to cover up my distended abdomen. I have some brown earring to go with it too. I think wearing that will work for me. The party turned out really good. Last count of the night was a little over fifty people. I did a little bit better with mingling this time too.

I think that I want to do something different for either the next party or the one after that. There is a comedy club on the west side. I think the name of the place is called The Village Idiots. I am going to ask Janet if she wants to go check it out with me. That might be a really cool party to host if I can work something out with the owner about the show tickets. From what I have seen on their webpage, it has the comedy show upstairs and a band and dancing downstairs.

I am going to call her right now and see what she is doing on Saturday.

"Hi Margie," Janet answered.

"Hi Janet, I wanted to know if you were doing anything Saturday night. There is a comedy club on the west side called The Village Idiots that I want to go check out. I am thinking about doing a party over there. I think it would be a lot of fun for everyone; but I want to see what it is like first before I talk to management about hosting and committing to doing a party there. If you aren't busy, would you want to come check it out with me?"

"Wow, Margie, what a great idea, but what would you do about the show tickets?"

"I haven't figured that out yet. Like I said, I want to see the show first, check out the club, and see if the place would be good for a party. Are you busy on Saturday or would you want to go check it out with me and let me know what you think about having a party there?"

"Sure, I will, I don't have anything going on Saturday."

"Good, do you just want to meet me up there or do you want me to pick you up?"

"Why don't you pick me up and we can go from here?"

"Okay, sounds good. I will pick you up around seven o'clock then, because the show starts at seven thirty."

"Okay, I will be ready."

"I will see you then. I have to get going here; I have a lot to do today. Bye."

"Bye."

I had been checking into other options as far as comedy clubs, but most of them either are just dinner and show; or they do not have live bands for dancing. The party would be very short and too expensive for most people to go too. This party is going to be a real challenge in working the issues out with management to make the party affordable and enjoyable for everyone to be able to attend. From what I have heard and seen online, The Village Idiots, looks like a place that I want to host the party at though. Like I said, it is going to be a real challenge putting this one together. I just hope that management will work with me on one; and that this is where I am going to be able to have the party.

This week has gone by so quickly. It is already Saturday and I am now getting ready to go pick up Janet and go out to watch the comedy show and just see how the place is. When we arrive there, we go upstairs and get a good seat to watch the show.

The comedians are a riot. I don't think that I have laughed so hard. We are having a blast tonight. This really is where I want to host a party. Now, I just have to somehow make it happen.

I called The Village Idiots on Monday afternoon and asked for the person that handles all of the parties and entertainment.

"Hi, this is Margie, I represent and host parties for a singles online site called Best Dating Ever. I am interested in hosting a party at your establishment."

"Hi Margie, let me get Carl for you, he is the one that you need to speak to about this."

"Okay, thank you."

Carl comes to the phone and says,

"Hi Margie, I understand that you want to host a party here."

"Yes, I came in with a friend on Saturday and saw the show. I have to tell you, I don't think I have enjoyed myself that much in a very long time."

"I am glad that you enjoyed the show."

"I really did. Is there a way that we could meet and discuss holding a party?"

"I don't think that I have ever had a singles party here. Sounds like it might be a lot of fun. Yes, I would like to sit down and talk to you about it. I have some time tomorrow afternoon, would four o'clock be okay with you?"

"That would be fine. I will see you then. Bye."

"I look forward to meeting you then Margie."

Tonight, I am going to be very busy trying to figure out how I can make this work. I have to write down all of my questions that I want to ask Carl. The biggest one is going to be if he would be able to waive the cover charge and the show tickets. I just don't even know if that would even be a possibility especially if he would allow the party to be on one of his busiest nights. And then there is the other question of possibly having one of the shows that night reserved strictly for my party. Yes, I know, I am going be asking a lot of Carl. However, let's face it, if I bring in a big enough crowd, he will make it up in drinks all night. I am going to try; the worst thing that he can tell me is that it isn't possible. I just hope that we can do this; I think it would be a blast for everyone. Definitely would be a party that no other host has ever had.

As I am writing down all of the questions, I am kind of getting excited. Each time I host one of these parties to, I feel like I am getting more confident. Meeting new people is slowly starting to get just a little easier each time. This is a good thing, not feeling so withdrawn all of the time like I had been. I can't get to comfortable yet and let my walls down to be open to get hurt again. I am just not ready yet.

Margie Garrett

It sure would be nice to be able to go on a date with a man though. It is one thing to do the parties and meet new people, but seems that I am still doing something wrong, because I am still not being asked out on a date. What am I doing wrong here? Probably nothing, but who knows.

As I take a break from writing down all of my questions for Carl, I went online to check and see if I have any messages. I do have a couple. One just happened to be from Mike, whom I met at the first party. He pretty much just commented on how good I looked and that it was a great party. He seems like a pretty nice guy; a little younger than me though. He asked me if I was going to be hosting another party soon. He gave me his phone number and said if I wanted to talk; to give him a call. I don't know if I want to call him though. I just answered him back and let him know that I am in the process of working and planning another party, but that I don't have a date for it yet. As soon as I do though, I will be posting it. I really did want to call him, but I couldn't bring myself to doing it yet, mostly in fear of being asked out. I want to go on a date badly, but I am so scared to go out with any man now after my last experiences in dating. I hope that I can get past this fear soon, because I don't want to be alone forever.

I would sure like to have a special man in my life. I just don't know if that is ever going to happen again in my lifetime. I sure hope so though. I am taking things so slow now, mostly concentrating on the parties. They seem to keep my mind off of everything else and very busy. This sometimes is a good thing; because I have less time to think of much of anything else going on around me. I just want to have fun and enjoy myself without all of the fear. Getting close to any man would result in dates which, right now, I have such mixed feelings about. Eventually, I know that I am going to have to go on a date again to get past all of the fears that I have. All men aren't the same, no more than women are to men. We are all different. We can't judge all men and women by a few bad experiences, and that is what I have to keep telling myself. I am sure that I will come across a good guy or two again. One of these days, I will find one; at least I hope that I will.

I have a phone call from Jim at Kitty Korner asking me if I know when I will be hosting another party with him. I told him that I am thinking probably the first of August. I said that I would get in touch with him closer to the date with an update on what is going on with the plans.

I have had yet another very busy day and am once again so very tired. I sure hope that I can get some solid sleep tonight, without all of the pain and vomiting. I need it, because I have so much to do tomorrow.

As I wake up with my cup of coffee, I need to go over all of these questions that I need to ask Carl this afternoon to make absolutely sure that I am not missing anything. This party is going to take a lot more convincing and planning to make this one work. I think that I have everything that I need to ask wrote down though. Now I can just relax and maybe take a nice hot shower; and then get ready to go meet with Carl at The Village Idiots.

As I am driving there, my brain is just racing with all kinds of thoughts and ideas. I am here in the parking lot. I took a deep breath and said to myself that I can do this. I can make this happen, and went in to meet with Carl.

I went up to the bar and said to the bartender,

"Hi, I am Margie; I am here to meet with Carl."

"Does he know you were coming in?"

"Yes, he asked me to meet him here around four o'clock."

"Okay, let me see if he is in yet."

"Okay, thanks."

"Can I get you a drink?"

"A Bud Light would be great."

"Coming right up."

"Thanks."

As Carl comes over to table he introduces himself. I thanked him for meeting with me.

"Margie, why don't you tell me a little about your parties and what you would need from me?"

"Well, like I had briefly told you on the phone, I am hosting singles parties for an online singles site called Best Dating Ever. I haven't had any parties on the west side; so I want to do one over here. I have parties that range anywhere from fifty to over one hundred and fifty members attending. I have them on Saturday nights just because most people are too tired on a Friday night after working all week. I came here Saturday to see the show upstairs and dancing. I really think that everyone would really enjoy themselves here. I have some questions for you though. First one is will I be able to book a party on a Saturday with a show strictly reserved for the party with the show tickets and cover charges waived?"

"Well, that is one of the busiest nights here. For me to do that, I would have to have the attendance from you. I can't if you are only going to have fifty when I can fit two hundred guests in for the show. There would have to be a minimum of a hundred. Do you think that is feasible?"

"Yes, I can do that I am sure. I will push for a full house of two hundred."

"In order for me to waive the tickets and cover charge, there will have to be a minimum of two drinks per person during the show and some food served. Can you guarantee that also?"

"Yes, I can."

"Then what I will do for you is book the first show for the night for your party which will be the seven thirty show. If your guests don't come until after the first show they will not get in free for the second, so you need to make sure they are aware of that. Also, the cover charge will be waived until nine o'clock, after that they will have to pay to get in."

"Fair enough Carl. When the show is over, they will want to continue the party downstairs with the band and dancing. Can I get any tables by the dance floor reserved for the party?"

"I can reserve your party some tables, but they will be in the back and not by the dance floor. That really is the best that I can do for you on that one. When were you thinking of having this party?"

"I need some time to put this all together and post it online; and have to allow enough time for people to decide and make sure that I have the attendance that you are asking for. I am thinking probably the middle of August. What are your thoughts and will that work for you?"

"Yes, that sounds good."

"Okay, well I will get back with you in a week or so and give you an update on everything. If this party works, I would like to host more parties here."

"They sound like a lot of fun."

"I try and have parties that people will enjoy and be able to meet others in a safe surrounding. And so far, they are working out well. I have seen a few connections. It makes it all worthwhile; all of the work that I do to organize them, when I see that happening."

"You are doing a good thing here and I am glad to have all of you come and party here."

"Thanks Carl. I have some work to do to get ready for it, so I better get going. Thanks again. I will get a hold of you next week."

"Okay Margie, it was nice meeting you. Take care."

I am so excited; walking out of there I had a huge smile on my face. This is going to be an awesome party. I am so glad that he was so cooperative with me on all that I want for the party. To be honest, I didn't think that he would agree to the tickets being waived, but I guess the two drink minimum was a workable solution. And that works for me, because I know that everyone will order that at the very least. This meeting went better than I had ever expected.

Now I have two parties planned, booked and posted. It is time for me to take time for myself and just relax again for a few days, especially since I am feeling so tired. I am having an awful lot of pain and vomiting from the Crohns Disease again. I think that all of the stress isn't helping matters any. It is time to take care of myself for a while and relax and get some well-deserved rest.

Over the next several days, I didn't do much of anything. I have no energy left in me at all. I feel totally drained. It seems like all I want to do is sleep these last couple of days. I would check my messages and respond to them, but that is about it.

I had a couple of messages. One was from Bob, just asking how I was doing and that he hadn't talked to me in quite a while; and the other one was from Mike. He asked me if I wanted to get together this Saturday and go to a club that has karaoke. I don't know what to say. I don't know if I am ready to go on a date again. I had met him and talked with him at a couple of the parties, but I am still not sure if I can do it. I am going to have to just think about that before I respond back. Bob has never asked me out, just always messages me though. I am not sure why, but he hasn't. The status on his profile states It's Complicated. I am not quite sure if that means that he is married, separated, or in a relationship. Who knows with the way some men are. Why they put on their profiles certain things. Confusing to me that is for sure.

I have decided to take a chance and go out with Mike this Saturday night. I sure hope that I don't regret my decision. I have to let someone know who I am with and where I am going though, just in case. I am also going to go to the store and get a little trial size bottle of hair spray that I can carry in my purse in case I need to defend myself. I hope that I don't need to with him.

Mike gave me his number before so rather than messaging him, I am going to call him.

He answered the phone,

"Hello."

"Hi Mike, this is Margie."

"Hi Margie, I was beginning to wonder if you were going to call me. I gave you my number the other day."

"Yes, I know. Sorry I didn't call you. It has been pretty crazy the last couple of days with the parties. I had to meet with the managers and clear some things up."

"How is the party planning going?"

"I have one planned over here at Kitty Korner for August fifteenth and the other one will be a different party on the west side. It is actually going to start with a comedy show."

"Well, that sounds like it will be a great party for the ones that can afford the ticket cost along with the drinks. I sure can't afford it though; so looks like I won't be able to go to that one."

"Sure you will because as long as you get two drinks during the show, there won't be any tickets to purchase. I got the show tickets waived."

"How did you manage to get the ticket cost waived?"

"The powers of persuasion," as I laughed.

"It doesn't matter how; the point is that I worked it out with the manager there."

"Well, I don't know how you managed it, but this party I have a feeling is really going to be a lot of fun."

"Yes, I think that everyone is going to have a really good time."

"Every party that you have put together and hosted has been good."

"That is a matter of opinion based on my emails."

"Why do you say that?"

"I have had a few pretty nasty messages from men who didn't have a good time for some reason."

"You do all that you can to put the parties together, it is up to them to have a good time. You can't do that for them."

"Try telling them that, some of them get downright rude to me."

"They have no right to be upset with you. Did you get my message earlier? Do you like karaoke, and would you like to meet me up there Saturday night?"

"Yes, that sounds like fun."

"Great, I will meet you up at the Do Drop Inn about nine o'clock then on Saturday night."

"Okay, I will see you then. Do me a favor though; can you remind me on Friday night? Things with planning and organizing these parties can get crazy at times. And issues with managers come up that I have to clear up."

"I will give you a call and remind you then."

"Okay, I will talk to you later."

"Bye for now."

I sure hope I am not making a big mistake going out with Mike.

Mike did call and left a message reminding me of tomorrow night's karaoke at the Do Drop Inn and said if I couldn't make it to please let him know; otherwise he would meet me up there.

And so Saturday afternoon, I called Janet and said,

"Hi Janet, I am crazy after all of my past dates, but that I am going to take a chance tonight. Mike asked me to go to karaoke."

"You aren't crazy, just please be careful. I am pretty sure that you will be fine with Mike though. Where are you two going? I will call your cell phone to check and make sure that you are all right."

"We are meeting up at the Do Drop Inn."

"Okay, well just try to relax and enjoy yourself. I don't have to worry about you drinking too much, you can nurse a beer all night," as she laughed.

"Yes, I am not a drinker, so no worries there."

"Okay, well I will give you a call later to check on you. Have fun and enjoy yourself."

"I will try too; I will talk to you later."

"Okay, bye for now."

I had decided that tonight I am just going to go comfortable and wear my jeans and black top, which is a first for him to see me this way. With the parties, I am always dressed up. I am not going to tonight though.

Here I go; I sure hope that he is different from the others.

"Hi Margie, I am glad that you came tonight."

"Thanks Mike."

"Did you get all of your song choices picked out?"

"Yes, he has them all."

"That's cool."

"Are you going to sing tonight?"

"No, I have never done karaoke. I will just watch all of you sing."

"You should try it."

"Maybe someday I will get brave but not tonight."

I sat there and we listened to others sing. I think that Mike may be up next. All in all, it was a good date. Mike is a really good singer too. It was a nice relaxing date and he was a gentleman the whole night. I was so relieved that he didn't act like the others. Janet did check on me to which made me more comfortable. Just knowing that she knew who I was with and where I was going helped a lot. I really appreciated her doing that.

I still wonder why Bob hasn't asked me out though. What is up with that? Sometimes, I just don't even want to try and figure out these guys.

The next party at Kitty Korner is in a few days now, so I called Jim to give him the head count.

Margie Garrett

"Hi Jim"

"Hi Margie, how are things going for the party?"

"They are going really well. I have about one hundred and forty seven coming so far."

"Wow, you were right, when you said that the parties would get bigger. I remember the first party you had around fifty or so."

"Yes the more people that comes to the parties, bringing with them their friends. That is why the parties tend to get bigger."

"These parties sure are helping my business."

"I am glad that they are. We have a lot of fun."

"You are a great hostess."

"Thank you Jim."

"You are very welcome Margie. Well, keep me posted on the party. I have another call so I will talk with you later."

"Okay, bye for now."

It is time for me to call Carl at the Village Idiots and give him an update to. And so I did and told him that I have about eighty two coming so far, but there still a couple more weeks for people to sign up and that I am sure that there won't be a problem with getting another twenty people.

I feel as though, sometimes, hosting these parties may be taking over my life. Don't get me wrong, I really enjoy all of the planning, organizing and hosting them along with all of the work that goes into them. After all, the parties are actually helping me regain my self-confidence back. That is a lot of the reason why I started doing them in the first place. Simply because I was so depressed and totally withdrawn from everyone and everything. I remember how I felt when I first started hosting these parties. I was terrified about meeting and talking to people that I didn't know. Don't get me wrong, I am still very nervous, but not nearly as bad as I use to be.

In checking my messages this morning, I have another message from a nineteen year old.

He says in the message to me,

"Hi beautiful, my name is Andy, do you want to have some fun tonight? Call me, here is my phone number."

I also have one from a twenty four year old that says to me,

"Hi gorgeous, I hope you don't mind the age difference, but I really like being with older women. They know what they want and teach me a lot."

I did answer this one back and said to him,

"Why in the world would you want to go out with someone your mom's age? Why not a woman only a couple of years older? We would have absolutely nothing to talk about."

He replied,

"We don't really need anything in common to have a night filled with fun and sex, now would we? Besides, I can go much longer than any guy your age."

I laughingly replied,

"Honey, I may be a lot older, but I am not dead and even you couldn't keep up with me."

"It sure would be a lot of fun trying, so what do you think?"

"I think you need to keep looking and dreaming."

I just stopped the conversation right there. That is sick; it would be like going out with my son. I can understand five or even ten years younger, but definitely not twenty five or thirty years younger. I think any man or woman that does that is just plain sick or very desperate for attention.

Margie Garrett

Tonight is the party at Village Idiots. I have one hundred and seventy six people signed, which is pretty close to a full house. Carl is very happy with the outcome. As I sit in the back of the room and watch everyone listen and laugh, it made me very happy to know that I organized this party. Everyone is really enjoying the show. The comedian was incredibly funny and Carl was so accommodating with everything that I needed tonight. After the show, everyone went downstairs and continued the party with the band and dancing. We all talked, mixed, mingled, and danced while having a great time. The next morning, I was curious to see what kind of feedback I had received from the party. I had so many that had thanked me for such a fun party. A group of us from the party had decided to meet up again next Saturday just to hang out and talk about all of our crazy dates that we have had, and just have some fun.

CHAPTER 13

Crazy Dates

I am still trying to get the group together for this Saturday just to hang out and tell stories. I am not sure how many will be able to come out though. It will be fun just to be able to hang out for the first time without all of the responsibilities of hosting.

Looks like a lot of us have showed up tonight. As we are all sitting around the table, we start talking about our crazy stories.

I had started out with a crazy date that I had,

"Several months ago, I went to meet with this guy Jack, he didn't look bad in his profile picture. He wanted to take me out dancing. He thought he was some kind of hot sexy dancer or something. I was so embarrassed. It was getting late and he was hungry, so he asked if I wanted to go get a bite to eat. I said sure. So we went to this restaurant down the street and ordered breakfast and when the waitress brought the food to the table, I looked up at him; and I could not even believe this, but he took his teeth out right in front of me."

Everyone at the table said

"Oh no," and started laughing.

"And then on top of that he was spitting as he was eating. I was so grossed out."

They were all laughing and Janet said,

Margie Garrett

"That is just plain sick. I don't know if this one is worse than yours; but one of my dates looked absolutely nothing like his picture. In his picture he was tall and muscular. Talk about not looking like his picture at all. He had no teeth on the one side of his mouth and was really overweight."

"Yuck." They all had said.

John said,

"I had been talking online to this hot beautiful lady for several weeks, so I decided to invite her over. She gets here, takes my hand, and pulls me right to the bed. Talk about not wasting any time. She stayed the night, but still, ghee. I guess that she knew what she wanted and was going to get it whether I wanted to or not."

"Wow, she is unbelievable." I had said.

Ron says

"Here is an even better one for you; I have been talking to this lady. She invites me over. Just as I arrive, and I didn't even think I had two steps in the front door when she gets a phone call. She tells me that I need to go into the backyard. I asked her why, and she said to me that it was her husband on the phone and he is out front. I told her that the only thing I see is two cop cars out front. She said, yes that is him. I asked her if she was kidding me and that this is a joke. She said no that is my husband. I said your husband is a cop, ghee. I climbed over the fence and ran like hell. I couldn't even believe it."

Sarah says,

"Here is a good one. This guy wanted to meet me at the mall. He said that it would be a good place to meet and he needed to get some shoes. So he found a pair and asked me if I like them. I said yes and suggested that he try them on. He started acting really weird when the worker came back with a pair to try on. I wondered why until he took his shoes off. I busted out laughing because his socks were full of holes and so long that they looked like one of those slinky toys. I couldn't help but to laugh."

We were all having such a great time tonight. We all had tears pouring down our eyes and my jaws were so sore.

George said,

"Okay it is my turn. I went to meet, what I thought, would have been a beautiful woman. She came in to the club and recognized me right away, but there was no way I would have ever known it was her. She came over and I was totally appalled, but didn't want to be rude. She was nothing like who she portrayed to be. I tried bowing out of the date, but I couldn't. She said that we should go outside and get some air. And so I did, having absolutely no idea, what was in store for me out there. When we got outside, her friend had been waiting for us. These two ladies were huge and my date says to me that we should go get a room and have some fun, as her friends hand starts to roam if you know what I mean. These ladies wanted to have a threesome with me. I just said that I didn't think so and that I think that I am just going to leave. I told them to have fun but count me out. And I bolted faster than you can imagine."

John says,

"Well, that is sick, but let's faces it; they wouldn't even get a meet with you if she had put her real picture up for you to see."

George said,

"No, you are right, she wouldn't. Looks are only skin deep, but come on, let's be serious here. She should have at least been honest."

Andy says,

"I am embarrassed, but I couldn't help this. I went to this girl's house for dinner with her and her parents. While I was eating I had gas really bad and had to fart. I tried really hard to hold it in or at least be quiet, but it didn't work."

Her father heard it and said

"Bandit" which was the dog laying under the table.

I was glad that he saved me on that one. We continued eating, but damn if I had to let loose again."

Her dad again said,

Margie Garrett

"Bandit".

This was good that the dog was hanging out under the table. This is horrible and this gas is killing me, I have to fart again. I let it rip" and her dad jumps up and said

"Bandit get out of there before he poops on you."

Oh my God, we were all laughing so hard that we had tears just rolling down our faces and everyone in the club is now staring at us, knowing how much fun we are having.

Donna says,

"Here is a sick one. I went to the grocery store with this guy to get a few things for a picnic. He picks up fruit punch which I hate. I am thinking, at this point, that there sure won't be much kissing going on tonight. He went to kiss me, and I pulled away and explained why. As sweet as this guy is, he went and brushed his teeth. Came back and started kissing me; you aren't going to believe this one. Half way through the kiss he freaking burps in my mouth and then tried to suck in his burp like he could take it back. Sick. It was disgusting."

I asked Donna,

"What did you do?"

"I pulled back and just pretended nothing disgusting just happened and promptly ended the date.

Kathy says,

"Okay, here is one for you. This is one of the craziest ones I have ever had. I had gone on a couple of dates with this guy already, but this one is funny as hell. I went over to his house to hook up. In the middle of having sex he completely stops moving. I didn't have a clue what was going on with him. I tried talking to him, then yelling. When I was just about ready to scream for some help he lets off this really loud snore. The jerk had fallen asleep right on top of me in the freaking middle of having sex with me."

Katie says,

"Of all dates to be asked out by a guy, he asks me out on Friday the thirteenth. He was a real jerk, but we are still happily married."

I said,

"Wow, what a day for him to ask you out, but awesome that you guys are still together."

"Thanks." Katie said.

Katie is a waitress and had shared that story with us when she overheard what we had been laughing about all night.

Andy said,

"Mine is pretty gross but funny. I had gone on several dates with this lady. Everything was going well. I decided that maybe tonight she would allow me to have sex with her, and in the middle, low and behold, does she fart right in my face, so much for the mood, because we both busted out laughing. I told her not to worry about it, but she was so embarrassed."

One of the other waitresses, Julie came over laughing and tells us her story.

"I had been dating this guy for a while. We were both still living with family members and so we had to behave. One night, he was dropping me off back home; we pulled off to the side of the road in a secluded area about a quarter mile from my home. It was dark and rainy and I could feel my adrenaline pumping as a few cars drove past unaware that we were making love behind the steamy windows. After we finished and got dressed, Jared started the car and started to pull back on the road. However, the car was stuck. We called the insurance company to have someone tow us out of the mud completely surrounding the car. About a half an hour later, the tow truck driver shows up and as Jared lies to him saying we made the wrong turn and were trying to get ourselves turned around."
The man stares at me and says,

"Julie, is that you?" "The guy was a friend from high school, whom I hadn't seen in almost seven years. He then recognized Jared; he seemed shocked but excited that we were dating. After the excitement wore down, my friend said to me,"

Margie Garrett

"Don't you just live up the street?" "Thereby, revealing that he didn't buy our story one bit. I was mortified."

I said to Julie,

"Oh my God, that is to funny, thanks for sharing your story with us Julie."

We are having so much fun and laughing so hard that by now others in the club were staring and laughing and now want to join in the fun with us. Not only did two of the waitresses share their story with us, but now others in the club are sharing their crazy date stories with us too.

This guy comes over to our table, none of us knows him, and says,

"Hi, I am Jack, I don't mean to interrupt, but I have been listening and laughing over there to all of your stories."

"Hi Jack." I said to him, as I introduced him to everyone at the table.

"Do you have a crazy date story that you would like to share with us?"

Jack says,

"Yes, here is one for you. I was set up with this lady that I never met before. My friend and his girlfriend brought her over to my house. I was on one sofa and she was on the other. I don't think that she said one word the entire night. It was so awkward. There was just total silence. Eventually, I just got up and went into the other room and watched some television."

"Wow, she was a whole lot of fun." I had said.

Jack says,

"Yes, I had a really fun date that night. Not!!! Would you guys mind if I joined you?" John asked,

"No, not at all, pull up a chair."

"Thanks."

Then another one came over to our table and said to us that it is really funny what we are talking about.

She said,

"Oh my name is Liz."

"Hi Liz." Don said.

Liz proceeds to tell us her story.

"On a first date with this guy, the beginning was okay, but once he became more comfortable, he told me that whenever he looked at his truck that he would get a hard on. Needless to say, I never let the second date happen."

I said to Liz,

"That is too funny, a hard on?"

Katie comes back over to the table and says to us,

"I have a quick minute, here is one for you. On my first date with this guy, there was a pretty romantic spot to sit, but of all places was in front of a monastery. We talked for a little while. He took my hand like a gentleman and said that I have very pretty hands. All of the sudden, the guy turned into a total sleaze ball. Without any warning at all, the jerk starts sucking on my fingers. I told him to stop so he let go of my hand, he then leaned forward closed his eyes and stuck his tongue out, all of this within the view of the monks bedroom. Talk about awkward. I put an end to the freak show right then."

Donna says,

"In front of a monastery, that is pretty funny. He couldn't have come up with a better spot than that?"

"Nope, I guess not."

Margie Garrett

John said,

"I have a friend who was virtually saying that there is no unattractive woman period. He ended up looking for a woman online. He came across this profile, but she had no photo. She is about two hours away. After talking with her, he had decided to drive two hours to meet with her. I guess that he felt that desperate. He came back with a pale face as he showed me the picture of the two of them. I almost fell off of my chair. She could have fit a couple of guys in her belly and then ask for dessert. She said in her profile a few pounds overweight. That gives the word "few" a whole new meaning."

"It sure does, I don't understand why people can't be honest about themselves in their profiles, especially if they intend on having that person drive two hours. That was just plain wrong." "It sure was."

George says,

"I have had a few, but usually revolve around woman using their high school pictures. They either haven't aged well, or they say that they are slim and show up in clothes that wouldn't fit a baby rhino." Everyone started laughing.

Another guy from the crowd comes over and says,

"I am having so much fun tonight listening to all of your stories that I just have to share one of mine. I was talking to this girl online for a couple of months. When I got myself a car and drove to see her. She didn't look anything at all like her picture. She almost looked like a linebacker. All I could think was that this is girl is uglier than a bull. Maybe, I can just see if I can get oral from her anyways tonight, and then in a few weeks just tell her that I found someone else. However, that was before I saw her penis through her clothes. I ran like hell out of her house and promptly drove away."

Janet says that she has another story for us,

"I go to get some Chinese food to take to the guys place. It was a very windy day and my hands were full. I go to open the storm door with my one hand trying to hold all of the food in the other hand. The wind takes the storm door and poof there goes the food all over my front, nothing like having wonton soup and steakkow all over your chest. I was so embarrassed."

We are all going to be going home tonight with sore jaws. This whole night has been full of fun and laughter.

Cool, Cheryl came after all. She comes up gives all of us a hug and jumps right in with a story and says,

"I placed an ad online and a guy answers. We make arrangements to meet and go see a movie. He comes to the door to pick me up, and, oh my God, it was like looking at Frankenstein with zits."

We all just started busting out laughing. I just knew that Cheryl would have a good one to share with us too.

"Come to find out he was a younger brother of a guy I went to school with. We go to the movie, find our seats and talk for a couple of minutes until the movie starts. Within about five minutes, the guy fell asleep. I'm thinking what the hell. The movie wasn't all that good, so I left half way through the movie. When I got back, he was still sleeping. When the movie ended he finally woke up and acted like he had been awake the whole time. I wasn't about to see him again."

I shared one of my stories with them,

"Okay, I have another one that a friend told me. She was out on a date with this guy. They spent the day together skiing, before they left the ski resort they went to get some hot coffee to warm up. After they had left the resort she needed to go find a restroom, but there wasn't one in sight. He proceeded to tell her to try and hold it; which she tried to but couldn't any longer. She asked him to pull off the road. She got out of the car to go pee. It was so slippery and so she knew that she needed to somehow support herself so she pulled her pants down to go and planted her butt against the back of the car. She was having some difficulties and was out for a while, so he called out to her asking if she was okay. Of course, she wasn't and she yelled back that she needed some help. When he went over there he started to chuckle because he could tell that her butt was frozen to the vehicle and she couldn't break free. He knew then what he needed to do. You got that right. He had to pee on her to set her free. They were both laughing afterwards. Well, I don't know about you guys, but I have had a blast tonight. I don't think that I have ever laughed so hard."

Margie Garrett

John said,

"Yes, this was a lot of fun. I am glad that we all were able to get together, just the group."

Janet asked me,

"Margie, do you have the next party scheduled yet?"

"Not yet, I have to talk to him tonight, which I probably should go do. It is getting pretty late. I will have it posted soon."

Janet says,

"Great, well I don't know about the rest of you, but I am going to head home. It is late and I have a long day tomorrow."

The party broke up. Everyone gave each other a hug and said good night and drive safely home. We really did have an incredibly funny night full of great stories. I am glad that we did this. I really need this.

CHAPTER 14

Depressed, Sick and All Alone

So after breaking up with Matt; after being in a relationship with him for several months, I find myself alone again. Once again; all of my self-doubt and insecurities are back, and up goes the walls surrounding me again. Not really knowing if I will ever find that special man to fill the void in my life. I am so tired of getting my heart broken. What is wrong with me? Why can't I find true love in my life?

I am almost ready to just say that dating just isn't worth the price that I pay each time I go out. I try so hard, but then maybe that is my problem. What should I be doing though? I just don't know anymore. There are so many dishonest and hurtful people in this world. I don't mean just men either, because there are a lot of woman that do the same to men.

We have heard stories from both men and women. Dating to me, seems to be nothing more than a never ending battle; and one that I am getting tired of and totally bored with. I have lost any enthusiasm now to go on any dates. I can't help how I feel. I wish that someone would just give me some insight on what in the world that I am doing wrong, because, I have absolutely no clue.

If nothing else, I have made some great friends. They have definitely become my second family and I love them so much. I am honored to have all of them in my life.

Over the next couple of days, I had become so withdrawn, depressed and in so much pain with the Crohn's Disease. Both Janet and John had been contacting me to see how I am doing, because they hadn't heard from me since the other night or seen me online either. I was just not really able to talk much to anyone.

Margie Garrett

I finally called John back, because to be honest, I needed a guy's point of view.

"Hi John."

"Where have you been Margie? I haven't heard from you lately. Are you okay?"

"Yes John, I am just really down. I don't understand what happened between Matt and me."

"It just didn't work out with you two, but you have to move on now."

"I know, not very easy when your heart has been broken time and time again. Why can't I find a guy who can love and respect me John? What is wrong with me?"

"There is nothing wrong with you. Speaking as a guy, we are all out for a challenge. You need to learn to give them a challenge and don't give in to their needs."

"To be honest, it is probably going to be a while before I even bother going on a date again."

"That might be a good idea to just step back and take a break for a while."

"I think that I am going to put all of my time and efforts into keeping myself busy with the parties right now again. That will help keep my mind off of everything else. Besides, my health right now isn't the best either."

"I take it your Crohns Disease is getting bad again?"

"Yes, so much for my brief remission. I never know from one day to the next how I will feel."

"Sorry Margie, I wish that there was something that would help."

"Just having supportive friends helps a lot."

"We are here for you if you ever need anything. I have to take care of my ladies you know."

"You are definitely a true friend John and I appreciate everything that you do."

"Well, kiddo, I have to get going here, I just pulled into work, so I will talk to you later."

"Okay, bye."

"Bye."

I had set up the next party for September twelfth at Kitty Korner; and posted it online this morning. Nothing else really needs to be done for it other than to monitor the site, and that only takes a few minutes during the day. I think that I am going to go get some rest. I haven't been feeling well at all these last couple of weeks. Maybe some rest will help. It certainly can't hurt me. That is for sure.

I took a pain pill and I went to bed. Sometimes they work, and sometimes they do absolutely nothing for me. Today, it seems like it worked really fast. I think that the minute my head it the pillow; I had fallen asleep. I was asleep the rest of the day and into the night.

For the next couple of days, my days and nights mostly consisted of sleeping. When things get this bad that is about all that I can do is sleep. I have no energy, ambition or strength to do anything else. Periodically, I do get this way. I guess it is my body's way of coping with the disease. It has been about three days now since I had gone online to check messages or talk to anyone. I haven't even checked the party thread to see how many have signed up. I have been so out of it. I know that the depression and stress isn't helping me either.

Sick and Tired
By Margie Garrett

With Crohn's Disease I am so sick
And Oh I am just so tired
Will the remission come quick?
I feel it is required

My stomach feels like a brick

Margie Garrett

The pain is by far desired
I just want to scream and kick
Can I just be retired?

The vomiting and diarrhea make me so sick
I don't want this, Crohn's you are fired
Crohn's you think you are so slick
Well you are not desired

Where is my control stick?
It is just so required
You may think you are slick
Just go away and become retired

As I eat my carrot and celery sticks,
My taste it has acquired
You will not win, you are so fired
So go away you dick
You are not desired

Shame on you Crohn's for making all of us so sick
We are just so sick and tired
Of all of your tricks
Yet some, despite you, are so admired

We don't want to be so sick
Nor be so tired
We wake up and want to kick
Most suffer as they have retired

Crohn's, you have made many so sick
Yet they are so inspired
You make me so sick
Please go, you are fired

I am planning on making this party different than the normal ones. At least I sure am going to try. It seems so pointless. Somehow, I really need to snap out of this depression and get my life back, because it is really getting bad; and pretty soon I won't be able to hide my true feelings anymore. All that I want to do these days is sleep. Then there are other days where I just want to curl up in a ball and die. I hate feeling this way. I feel like I have absolutely nothing to look forward too, every day just being the same as the day before, nothing different.

There is nothing new or exciting in my life, nothing at all. The only time that I go outside these four walls is when I am hosting the parties; and I am working them. I watch everyone else have a good time, envious of all of them.

The depression is really taking hold of my life right now. I know I am the only one that can change how my life is. I just don't know how to. Maybe I am not supposed to have happiness and love in my life. Please tell me that I am wrong. I feel like I am just a robot going through the motions of living, but not really living. This isn't what life is all about, it can't be.

As I check my messages again, I have one from a guy. I check his profile; it says he is single and looking for a long term relationship. I like his profile, but how honest and sincere is it. Or is he just another guy to mess with my head. His profile picture is good. He says that he is five foot eleven and about two hundred pounds and muscular.

I figured that I really don't have anything to lose, so I replied back. We talked over the next couple of days and he finally asked me if I would like to meet him for coffee.

I can't believe that I am doing this, but I can't judge all men by a few. I just hope that his profile is true and not a bunch of lies. I am so uncomfortable with meeting any man now. Never knowing whether I will be safe or not. This, too, was a total flop for a date. He lied in so many ways on his profile. I am so over it all. I am done with dating. I will continue to talk to the ones that I had been talking with online, but no more dates. I refuse to be hurt, heartbroken and lied to anymore. I am done playing all of their games. I just can't and won't do it anymore. I am pretty much just keeping my lonely sad life to myself. After all, most guys don't want to hear about all of the drama. Which I sure have enough of in my life right now.

I hadn't heard from Bob in several months until now. He, once again, just contacted me to see how I am doing. As much as I don't like lies, I lied to him and said that I was great. Yeah right!! We talked for a few minutes and as usual that was about it. He still hasn't asked me out on a date.

I continue to check my messages only to get the same kind of men. Old, young, in a relationship, it's complicated, or the big one the guys is freaking married but looking for some fun on the side. Do I answer them anymore? I don't like to be rude; that just normally isn't me. However, right now, I just don't really care what any of them think of me right now. Especially, when the impression I get from all of the messages is that they are just looking for one thing and they aren't going to get it from me.

To be honest, I don't think that I have answered one message or accepted one friend request in the last several days now. I just don't care anymore. I have lost all interest in the dating scene. Especially, when I get messages like this one I just read tonight. Listen to this message,

"Hi gorgeous, my name is Mark. Like my muscles? I work out all of the time. You look so edible. I could pleasure you all through the night and all day tomorrow. I want to taste your sweetness. What do you say? Would you like that? I bet you have never had a night like I will give you; including a full body massage and with my tongue too. I am waiting to hear your answer." Now how sick is that.

See now why I have lost all faith and interest in men. With all of my past experiences of attempted rape, rape, physically beat, harassed, verbally abused and stalked by men, it really takes the fun out of dating. I just don't know which man I can trust and which I can't. I don't feel safe with any of them anymore. I just don't.

I am now starting to have some issues with the online dating site and my parties. It seems that because Jim at Kitty Korner had been taking care of my tab as a host for the parties, someone was very jealous and thought that he shouldn't have been. I know who it was too; it had to have been Andrea. She was always complaining and causing some problems, but I never thought that she would do anything like this, to report a bunch of false accusations. She reported that for every party I was hosting, I was getting a kickback on the profits for the night.

Over the next several weeks, all I did was try to defend myself, but they were not listening or responding to my messages at all. Why would she do this to me? I have never done anything hurtful to her or anyone else. I worked hard to host these parties, mostly, for all of them. All I ever got out of them was a couple of drinks and maybe a salad from management, surely not a kickback that she accused me of getting.

I had parties booked for September and October. I managed to be able to host most all of them accept for one. I received a message from the site telling me that I could no longer host any parties, post anything in the forums for the next two years. They had suspended all of my privileges without any consideration of the truth.

CHAPTER 15

Where is The Love?

I now, have no more parties to host, and without being able to sign up for any parties and have absolutely no dates either, I am really feeling all alone again. This truly is the story of my life. I should be used to this by now though. I, now, sit in what feels like a cocoon with nowhere to go and nothing to do. I have no more planning, organizing or meetings with club managers. I refuse to go on any dates, for fear of letting my walls down and being hurt again. Having way too much time on my hands to dream about what could be, but probably will never have in my life. A life full of dreams that probably will never come true, they are nice dreams though.

I lay in the bed, I cry and I sleep. I eat very little, because I just want to die. What do I have to live for? I live a life of being sick with this horrible disease and loneliness. This isn't living; I just exist in a world that I don't want to be in anymore. I have become extremely depressed and have had suicidal thoughts, not that I could or would ever harm myself. I am just so unhappy with my life. Knowing how I feel about dating men and being all alone as a result of my decision sure isn't helping my depression or my Crohn's at all. I have pretty much isolated myself from the world.

Out of curiosity, I went and checked messages. I have one from Bob again. I don't know what is up with him. He just seems to contact me sporadically every so often. He just checks to see how I am doing and what is new with me. He has yet to ever ask me out on a date. I wonder if he ever will. I replied back that there was nothing new and that I am doing okay. That was all he had to say. He sure doesn't talk much, but I still feel that there is something that he wants to say to me, but never does. I am not sure what it is about him, but I don't ignore his messages like I do all of the others.

Much to my surprise, Bob left a message for me, asking to meet me. It has been several months of waiting and hoping that he would. Now that he has, I am now terrified, because I want him to like me for me and not want to take me out for other reasons. I honestly think that if that was the only reason he wanted to meet with me, he would have asked me out long ago when he first had contacted me. We hadn't decided whether we were just going out for coffee or what we were going to do. We had talked on the phone over the next few days. Bob told me that he has two tickets to the Auto Show for this Saturday and asked me how I would like to go with him. I had said that I would like that. I didn't hear from him again for another few days or so.

We did go to the Auto Show on Saturday. As we were walking, I took Bobs' hand and continued walking. I really didn't know if he would pull away from me. To be honest, I really didn't even realize I had taken his hand. It just happened. It was probably about the best date that I had in a very long time. The real question here is how Bob felt about me. Would he want to see me again? All that I know is that at this very moment, I am happy. For that I am grateful. One day of happiness is better than none. I just hope that the happiness continues. I guess that time will tell. Now I just wait to see what happens with us.

EPILOGUE

Depression and Anxiety can affect how I feel from day to day. Anxiety is associated with threats of danger, where anger could be from someone hurting my feelings. Depression could be triggered, as in my case, of losing my marriage and sadness and also having to deal with my Crohn's Disease on a daily basis.

Depression can also be caused from ultimately dangerous encounters. There are many ways of facing dangerous encounters. Some of them may be from driving down the road and encountering a dangerous driver not paying attention to their own driving which can cause an accident, or there could be a situation where you go on a date with a man or woman and it turns out to be potentially with a very dangerous person who might attack you causing danger and anxiety. There could be financial and emotional and health situations that can cause major depression that could ultimately result in suicide. These are all dangerous encounters that some have to deal with on a daily basis. In my situation, my dangerous encounters are my health with my Crohn's Disease and Depression and I have had some seriously dangerous dates.

The statistics for depression are astounding. Here are some of the facts. Statistics show that approximately eighteen million American adults suffer from a depressive disorder. That is over nine and a half percent of the United States population, which includes major depressive disorder, dysthymic disorder along with bipolar disorder. Shocking as this is, our pre-schoolers are the fast growing for antidepressants. Statistics show that over a million which is approximately four percent are clinically depressed.

Not only have I had to deal with the depression in my life for various reasons, but the Crohn's Disease has really taken a toll in my life too. In my battle with my Crohn's Disease, I realize that I am definitely not alone. There are so many people in this world suffering with some form of IBD (Inflammatory Bowel Disease), Crohn's Disease and Colitis. I never knew how many until my research about my disease began. The statistics to me were shocking. It seems that one out of every five hundred people will suffer

Margie Garrett

from Inflammatory Bowel Disease which is over five hundred forty thousand people in the United States alone. Of these, there are so many that are children suffering.
Will I ever find health and happiness in my life? I know that living with Crohn's Disease, Colitis and Depression is not easy. I struggle with my health every day since being diagnosed. Most people have no idea what a struggle it is to live a life of pain every single day. And then you add in all of the other symptoms, makes it a real challenge to keep a positive attitude with life. Trying to bring a little happiness into my world certainly would help my moods, but I just don't know if that will ever happen for me. I struggle every day to be stronger than the day before.

I am thankful every day that I have the support of others that have the disease, because at least I have someone to talk to that can totally relate to what I am dealing with. We are here to support each other, both with the disease itself and all of the emotional problems that go along with it. I can be up one day and totally down on others. It is like a vicious circle that never ends.

I will never be happy being blessed with this horrible disease and what it is doing to my body. I have to find happiness in other ways with my life. I know that. I had hoped that I could find that special man to share my life with. I do the best that I can to not let my Crohn's and Depression rule my life, the disease sure doesn't make it easy to live my life the way that I want to live it though. Can I find some happiness in other areas of my life? I am sure that I can. I am just not quite sure how I will do that yet. I sure am going to try though. I won't let this disease or depression rule or win over my life. I can't and I won't.

HERE IS A SNEAK PEEK TO

In Hope of a Brighter Future
Sequel to Vicious Circle

I wake up in the morning to just another day of gloom. Looking at these four walls has now become my life, that and sitting or hovering over the toilet. What a life? Not the life that I would have chosen for myself. I have to snap out of this and change my attitude and outlook on life. Maybe, there is a reason for the life I have been dealt. Am I here to help others deal with their feelings of loneliness, helplessness, and feeling so hopeless over their daily living of being constantly in pain and ill? I just don't know.

Even if that is the case and the reason, then I need to fix my own attitude and outlook on life, or I certainly can't help others to deal with their daily challenges in life. I just can't.

Over the next couple of weeks, I try very hard to change the way I have been thinking about how my life is just not worth living anymore. I want and I need to be loved and be happy and right now I don't really feel either. All that I feel is pain and suffering, and this is just not how I want to live my life. I may not be able to change or dismiss the chronic pain from my life, but I can certainly change how I deal with it all, and how I want my future to be. I wish someone would just help me wake up from this darkness that I am living in right now.

I heard from Bob today. I sure needed to hear a friendly and caring voice today, with as down as I am. He always seems to know how to put a smile on my face, even if it is only for a few minutes. It sure does help my mood.

Then, I think about all of my health issues and how it might affect a relationship with a man, and wonder if I ever will have a relationship again. Let's face it, most people shy away from anyone that have any kind of health issues, they just don't want to take that on in their lives and I really couldn't blame them. It is a lot to deal with.

Over the next couple of days, I had been vomiting so violently, that I started vomiting up dry blood, it looks like coffee grounds. This tells me, that the blood is dry and is way up in my digestive system somewhere. I became scared and decided that I better just go to the emergency room at the hospital and get checked out. The exam was horrible. To see if the bleeding had stopped, the doctor had to put a tube down my nose to start flushing out to see if there happened to be any more blood there, which luckily there wasn't. It was horrible though, not a procedure that I ever want them to do on me again.

The doctor just gave me some medicine to help with the nausea and vomiting and told me to make sure that I keep the appointment with the gastroenterologist next week, and sent me home, and went straight to bed, wishing that I had a loving man to hold me through all of this, but I just don't think that it will ever happen in my life. I felt absolutely horrible and once again still with no answers. I feel like the doctors are just all passing the buck to another one, because they don't know what to do or think.

For the next couple of days, I just lay in bed depressed, with nothing but days of vomiting, diarrhea and pain in the abdomen and lower back. I feel so all alone, with no one to hold me, comfort me and love me. Why? Am I that horrible of a person, or is it just because of the constant chronic illness that I bear, that I can't seem to get close to anyone? Will I ever be able to live a somewhat normal life, because I can't really stand this life, at least not the way I am living, if you want to call this living? I just have to believe that a miracle will happen at some point that will change things around for me, and that I will figure out why this has happened to me.

As far as relationships in my life, I don't know how or if I will ever find that special man either, one that will be able to handle all of my illnesses. Could Bob be the one man that can make all of my dreams come true? He sure seems to care enough to contact me and check to see how I am doing. I would like to believe that he could be. Could there be a connection between the two of us at some point? I can only hope that there could be, but time will tell